DATE WITH DESTINY

The Untold Story of
United Flight 1175
AND THE MAN WHO SAVED IT

BY CAPTAIN CHRISTOPHER BEHNAM
——— THE FLYING LION ———

Kidsocado International Publishing

Serial Number: P2546190218
Title: Date with Destiny
Sub Title: The Untold Story of United Flight 1175
Authors: Captain Christopher Behnam, The Flying Lion
ISBN: 978-1-77892-224-4
Metadata: Biography, True Story & Adventurous Aviation
Book Size: 6 by 9 Inches, Paperback
Pages: 260
Publish Date: February 2025
Publisher: Kidsocado Publishing House

Copyright @ 2025 By Kidsocado Publishing House
All Rights Reserved, including the right of production in whole or in part in any form.

Kidsocado Publishing house
Vancouver, Canada

WhatsApp: +1 (236) 333 7248
Email: info@kidsocado.com
https://kidsocado.com

Contents

Foreword 7
By Tony Kern 7
Chapter 1, 2018 11
Chapter 2, 1965 14
Chapter 3, 2018 21
Chapter 4, 1965 26
Chapter 5, 2018 35
Chapter 6, 1972 48
Chapter 7, 2018 56
Chapter 8, 1974 61
Chapter 9, 2018 70
Chapter 10, 1972 78
Chapter 11, 2018 86
Chapter 12, 1975 93
Chapter 13, 2018 98
Chapter 14, 1973 103
Chapter 15, 2018 114
Chapter 16, 1976 118

Chapter 17, 2018 139

Chapter 18, 1979 150

Chapter 19, 2018 156

Chapter 20, 1979 160

Chapter 21, 2018 169

Chapter 22, 1980 178

Chapter 23, 2018 188

Chapter 24, 1983 193

Chapter 25, 1985 206

Chapter 26, 2020 217

Chapter 27, 1987 – Present 221

Epilogue 243

My Message: Do Not Delay Joy 243

About the Author 253

Captain Christopher Behnam 253

Acknowledgments 255

To my mom and dad, and my children.

"This is the true joy in life—being used for a purpose recognized by yourself as a mighty one. Being a force of nature instead of a feverish, selfish little clod of ailments and grievances, complaining that the world will not devote itself to making you happy. I am of the opinion that my life belongs to the whole community, and as long as I live, it is my privilege to do for it what I can. I want to be thoroughly used up when I die, for the harder I work, the more I live. I rejoice in life for its own sake. Life is no brief candle to me. It is a sort of splendid torch which I have got hold of for the moment and I want to make it burn as brightly as possible before handing it on to future generations."

George Bernard Shaw—

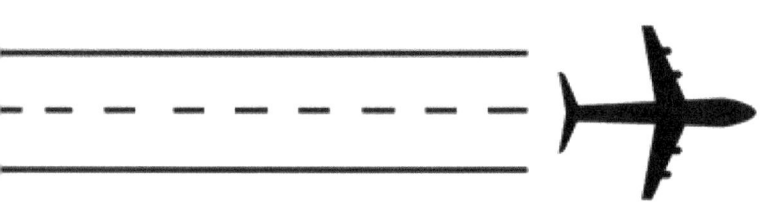

Foreword

By Tony Kern

On the wall in my office, I have one of my favorite quotes from one of my favorite historical icons, Sir Winston Churchill. It reads:

> **"To each there comes in their lifetime a special moment when they are figuratively tapped on the shoulder and offered the chance to do a very special thing, unique to them and fitted to their talents. What a tragedy if that moment finds them unprepared or unqualified for that which could have been their finest hour."**

At 11 a.m. (local time) on February 13, 2018, Captain Christopher Behnam was commanding United Airlines Flight 1175 in a Boeing 777. He and his crew were experiencing a routine flight from San Francisco to Honolulu when he heard a loud bang accompanied by multiple warning indications and a violent shaking of the aircraft. He would soon discover they had experienced a catastrophic failure of the number 2 engine and had lost 80 percent of their thrust. They were also experiencing significant drag induced by the damage to the surrounding area. Beneath him were 200 miles of open ocean between their location and the safety of the Hawaiian Islands.

The story you are about to read is Captain Behnam's first-person account of how he and his crew brought the stricken aircraft and 381 souls to a safe landing an hour later. Descending through thick cloud cover, barely able to read their instruments, the crew bonded in ways that, tragically, other airline crews in past events were not able to do.

But this is not just a story of a miracle recovery by a well-trained crew, it is much, much more. This is a story of what Churchill referred to as the chance to do "a very special thing, unique to them and fitted to their talents." As you will soon learn, Captain Behnam had been preparing his entire life for just this moment. From escaping from political upheaval in Iran as a child to finding his way to the United States, learning a new language, and climbing his way to the pinnacle of the aviation world, Captain Behnam practiced professional acumen and discipline to become the "Flying Lion."

But it was far more than professional training that prepared him for this moment. A few years ago, I had the pleasure of meeting Captain Behnam and hearing his story. Not just the flight on that fateful day, but how he lives his life. In his words, "seeking nature's balance." From rock balancing ("Everything has a center, even a dead rock") to martial arts (he is a third-degree black belt), to sailing ("where the machine and nature combine in balance to propel you forward"), I discovered a man with a deep and thoughtful process for living—one that found its way into the cockpit that afternoon. I immediately asked him to write his book. This is the result of that conversation.

Captain Behnam is not only seeking balance in his life as a whole, but also seeking precision and continuous improvement in his chosen profession. After more than three decades as a professional pilot, his passion for excellence burns brightly for all to see. This is rare in nearly every industry, where many become self-satisfied and complacent, becoming stagnant professionals who no longer grow and often become cynical in the late stages of their careers.

So this is not just a book for pilots, although every pilot should read it. It is a book for anyone seeking balance in their own lives—preparing for that moment when they are "figuratively tapped on the shoulder and offered the chance to do a very special thing." Dedication to family, passengers, his colleagues, and his profession—all these attributes came together when they were most needed, resulting in a flawless performance under incredible pressure and high stakes. We can learn much from Captain Behnam about how we can all prepare for the challenges in our own lives, so that when we are tapped on the shoulder, we too can respond with our "finest hour."

Chapter 1

2018

It's February 13, 2018. United Flight 1175 will leave San Francisco on time. It's a beautiful sunny day. As I drive to the airport, there's not a cloud in the sky. Although I live in Sacramento, I spent the previous night in Sausalito on my sailboat to cut down on commute time and to ensure a good night's sleep. It's about an hour and a half to SFO from Sacramento, but with traffic that can easily double. As I drive to San Francisco, I think of my father, who's struggling with stomach cancer. I recall the times we've spent together and look forward to the times that'll come. My flight is to Hawaii, one of my favorite routes. I love it there—the culture, the religion, the people, the foods, tastes, sounds, smells, everything. It'll be nice to land.

I arrive at the airport, settle in, and prepare for the flight.

I meet with Paul Ayer, my copilot for the day. We've never met before, but that's common. Aviation isn't the kind of work where you'll often see the same faces every day.

On the plane, we complete the required paperwork and continue to preflight checklists. Paul does a walkaround of the plane. Starting at door one on the left side, he walks clockwise around the Boeing 777. It's a massive plane. He checks the engine cowling. All the fasteners are closed. He checks the blades. He spends some time there. If there's a nick, even if it's as small as a dollar coin, the flight is a no-go. But the blades look good. Paul continues his inspection. He checks the tire pressure, the wheels, the steering mechanism, anything that can be visually checked. If something's wrong, he'd let a mechanic know and the problem would be seen to. But there's no need for that. So far, everything's good.

He continues around to the back of the plane. He checks the static ports and pitot tube probes, which measure air velocity. The covers are off, and the probes are unobstructed. Paul continues around the leading edge of the plane. He makes sure that there are no hydraulic leaks. Paul finishes his walkaround and heads back to the cockpit.

The first officer, Ed Gagarin, is also there. Ed is a newly qualified pilot for the 777. He was just a passenger on the flight, but I have asked him to ride in the jump seat since the flight is full and there are no seats for him in the back. We go through the final checklists and program the computer with the flight plan. I tell operations that we're 10 minutes from pushback. I brief Chief Purser Cecilia, the head flight attendant, about our flight time and the expected altitude and weather toward Honolulu. She heads off to her duties. We taxi the plane out on runway 28-left. I ask Paul if he'd like to fly the first leg. He does, and agrees. I'll be handling communications and navigation. I brief the passengers for our five-hour flight. It's still a beautiful morning. We take off and all 381 souls on board leave San Francisco behind.

Chapter 2

1965

When I was 6, I saw my father dragged away, beaten and bloody. I lived with my four sisters and my parents in Tehran, Iran. Back then, it was like the Paris of the Middle East. The days felt safe. People were friendly. Doors were kept unlocked. Our summers were spent in the countryside, in Takor, where my dad had bought a piece of property and built a modest two-bedroom, two-bathroom house. It was a good life.

There were 20 or 30 houses on our street. They were all connected, and they looped around in a cul-de-sac. In the back, each house had its own garden, or courtyard, where there'd be a little pond or fountain or swimming pool. This was no suburban sprawl. The homes were like the row houses of New York City or Washington, D.C., with entrances on the sidewalk that opened straight into the house itself. That is where my sister Goli, my elder by just under a year, and I were standing, in the nonexistent mudroom, when she opened the door and our lives changed forever.

Our mother was out getting groceries. The two of us were home alone, playing hide-and-go-seek. I'd just settled into my spot when there was a knock at the door.

"Hey, come on out. There's somebody at the door. Come on out," my sister said.

I came out from my hiding spot. The game was over. We had guests.

We approached the door. My sister was tall enough, taller than me at the time, to reach the doorknob. She cracked open the door, just enough so we could see outside.

The hot air swept in. Two men stood in front of our home. They looked friendly. They had big smiles, and they greeted us warmly and politely. We were more cautious. They introduced themselves as our uncles and told us that they were looking for our father. They chatted with us for a bit. They said that they were supposed to have met him, but that they'd grown concerned when he didn't show up. They were wondering where he was. They asked if he was home and, if he was, if they could see him.

Chapter 2

We didn't know any better. We were young and innocent.

My sister did all the talking. I watched from behind. She told them that he wasn't at home. They asked where our mother was, and Goli told them that she was out of the house as well. They asked again if we knew where our father was. My sister pointed across the street, at a home a few houses up on the opposite side of the road. She told them that he was at his mother's home. They thanked us and headed across the street.

We watched as they approached our grandmother's home. More men appeared. They all went inside. There was muffled commotion within. We weren't sure what was happening until it spilled out onto the street. The men emerged, dragging our father behind them. There was shouting and screaming. My grandmother's voice broke through the cacophony. "What are you doing?" I heard her cry. "Don't take him! Don't take my son!"

We couldn't avert our eyes.

Unable to walk on his own, our father was dragged by four or five guys on each of his arms. They placed him in handcuffs, threw him in a car, and drove him to Evin Prison.

Those moments are seared into my memory. The sounds, the screams, the smell of the dirt and sweat filling the air. I still remember what my father was wearing: a white shirt and grey pants.

I was in utter disbelief. I couldn't believe what had just happened. A flurry of questions rushed through my mind. *Why are they doing this to my dad? What did he do wrong? Is he a bad man? Is he a thief? Is he a criminal?* I couldn't even begin to fathom that something like what I just saw was possible, let alone that it could happen to my father.

The car with our father disappeared around the corner. We didn't know what to do or say. We were in shock. I wasn't screaming. I hadn't fully processed what had happened. It all occurred so fast, in maybe 10 or 20 seconds between the time they dragged him from our grandmother's house and when they drove off.

Our father was gone.

Alone, we waited for our mother to return from shopping. We sat in silence. There was no way we could go back to playing. My sister began to cry. I felt the same. My insides were tied in knots from concern. I didn't know what to think or do or say. I didn't know how to comfort her but there wasn't much I could do or say. We wanted our father back.

It felt like an eternity but, finally, my mother knocked on the door. We ran to her and grabbed her hands and legs and held on. My sister was bawling. When I finally told my mother what happened, or at least what I understood of it, it was her turn to collapse. The groceries tumbled to the floor. She could hardly stand. She held us tight. "I'm sorry," she said. "I'm so sorry." She said it again and again and again.

We kept asking her what happened.

"Is our father a good person?"

"Why did they hurt our dad?"

She told us that everything was going to be okay. Our father was a good person. I asked her if they took him away because he was bad. As far as I was concerned at that age, that's what happened to bad people; they got taken away. My mother told me, again, no, he just believes in certain things that the government didn't want him to.

Later that afternoon, maybe an hour or two later, my grandmother came over. My mother wanted to know exactly what happened. Our grandmother told us the whole story of how the SAVAK, the private police during the Pahlavi dynasty, forced themselves into her home, how there was a fistfight that ended with our father being dragged from the house. Even now, I can close my eyes and go right back to those moments. It's the type of negative anchor that makes you think about the injustices done to people just for their belief system.

In my eyes, my father was the most democratic person I have ever met in my life. Even after his torture, the pulling of his fingernails, the shocks to his groin, he still loved his country. He wanted Iran to be free, prosperous, and democratic. He wanted the Iranian people to be educated and to become the pride of the world. He wanted a free republic. He didn't believe in a dictatorship or monarchy. He believed that Iranians should decide for themselves.

Later, my mother told me that my father knew that they might come and arrest him at any moment. That's why he was at our relatives' homes. He was trying to avoid the SAVAK.

These years were incredibly difficult for me, my mother, and my sisters. This wasn't the only time my father would be arrested. There were nights when we'd wake to people in our home, ransacking the house, looking for my father's books and belongings. One night, when my uncle was with us, the SAVAK came while we were all asleep. My uncle told them that there were kids asleep inside the home, but they didn't care. They came, ransacked, and took documents and books. We were terrified, but there was nothing we could do.

We counted the days until my father came back. He was a teacher, a professor, and a chemist. His father had died when he was very young, and he had to put himself through school while taking care of his brother and mother. Normally, he'd leave in the morning to go to work and he'd return at night. It was strange not having him around. There were many times when we'd ask our mother when he was coming back. She reassured us. She told us he was fine, that he was safe, that she was in contact with him, that she'd visited him, and that he'd be released from prison soon. She promised us again and again that he was not a bad man. And he wasn't.

He would be gone for almost a year. He would continue to be beaten and tortured, his testicles zapped with electricity. The only crime he had committed was loving his country.

Chapter 3

2018

It's a beautiful day in San Francisco, roughly 70 degrees outside. Visibility is about 10 miles. The climb was unremarkable, which is a good thing. Flying over the Pacific Ocean, we reach cruise altitude. On the way to Hawaii, we're in the middle of the largest body of uninterrupted water between two points in the world. While Hawaii to Tokyo is technically a farther total distance, you have the Midway Islands and plenty of other places you can land in between. But from San Francisco to Hawaii, there is only pure, open emptiness.

We reach the point of equal time in the flight. The point of equal time, or PET, is the point where we're no longer able to backtrack or divert our flight path should something go wrong. And if God forbid something should, landing on the water is barely an option. You don't want to land a Boeing 777 on water. Imagine hitting a solid object with your car at 500 miles per hour. If you land in in 10-foot waves in the Pacific Ocean at 200 miles per hour, there will be little left of that airplane. In other words, to land a Triple Seven on the water is to crash it. Chesley "Sully" Sullenberger was lucky to land on the Hudson River where the waves were microscopic in comparison to the 10- to 20-foot waves of the Pacific Ocean.

Midflight, we hit some routine turbulence and decided to go to a lower altitude. It's still bumpy, so up we go from flight level 38 (38,000 feet) to 36,000 feet. The seatbelt signs turn off. We're about 200 miles from Honolulu and nearing the top of our descent—the end of the cruise phase of a flight and the beginning of the descent phase before approach and landing—so Paul and I begin to brief our approach for runway 4R into Honolulu. We do our descent checklist. Everything's in order. I get up and go to the lavatory and return a few minutes later to a calm cockpit. I settle back into my seat. My hands are a few feet from the controls and the seats are reclined. It looks like it's going to be a nice, easy landing.

When I'm in the sky, everything slows down for me. When you're on the ground, the chaos of the world consumes you. The news. The media. Celebrity gossip and political drama. A country's president consumes the news cycle yet again. A Kardashian has a baby. A celebrity proclaims that a new laxative tea is the secret to their weight loss. But up in the sky, everything is different. There's a beautiful, powerful stillness to it. It shifts your perspective. At a thousand feet up people are just dots. At 5,000 feet you can't even make out your own home. It's swallowed by the vastness of the ground below. The higher you go, the more of the Earth you see. Details melt away into a vast geography. Earth, and the life on it, go from micro to macro. On the ground, people follow their routines, run between rooms, juggle paperwork and phone calls, or sneak in sessions at the gym before heading home to dinner and sleep. Then they wake and the cycle begins again. But up here, the world below is of no mind. After 40 years of flying, each time I take to the sky, I'm still humbled by the majesty that nature has laid out beneath me. Sometimes when I'm not working, I get in a single-engine airplane and take to the sky. There I'm free as a bird. I fly over the mountains at 500 feet, 1,000 feet, over populated areas, which is the lowest you can go. Sometimes I take my girlfriend. We fly out to Lake Tahoe or Truckee, spend the day there, and fly back at night, taking in the sunset on the way home.

Then: An explosion almost catapults my head against the glareshield. It's as if we hit a brick wall at 550 miles per hour.

The plane pitches, yaws, and starts to roll to the right. The aircraft violently shakes and vibrates.

The autopilot and autothrottle disconnect and the plane tilts to a 45-degree bank. Symmetrical thrust is gone.

We're flying a damaged aircraft, and we have no idea of what's wrong. The noise in the cockpit is deafening. We have to shout to be heard.

I must control the aircraft.

Triple Sevens are massive, and when one of its two engines dies, that side (in this particular aircraft) goes from 90,000 pounds of thrust to nothing while the other side maintains its full thrust. This extreme imbalance makes controlling the aircraft extremely difficult.

Time in the cockpit begins to stretch. Seconds elongate into an eternity.

My concern is singular: landing.

I visualize a smooth touchdown, the landing gear hitting the runway, peaceful and crisp.

Someone once asked the tennis player Andre Agassi how he could hit a small ball coming at him at a hundred miles per hour. He answered that to him it wasn't a small tennis ball, but rather he perceived it as a giant basketball coming at him in slow motion. At his level of skill, he was operating at a different perception of scale. Now so am I.

I can see Paul and Ed's hands and mouths moving, but it feels as though I'm in a different dimension.

Thoughts rush to mind.

What is happening?

The airplane might be falling apart.

How do I keep the wings level?

We may have to ditch it in the water.

How do I land this plane?

Can we make it to Honolulu?

There are 381 people on board, 381 souls.

Is she going to stay airborne and flyable?

How do I control and land this plane?

How do I land this plane?

Chapter 4

1965

My father never resented my sister for what she did, but she still does not forgive herself for telling those men where he was.

In the tumultuous history of Iran, my father, Ali Asghar Behnam, played a significant role as a member of the National Front Party, opposing the rule of Mohammad Reza Pahlavi, the Shah of Iran. During my adolescence, his political activism landed him in prison several times.

The National Front Party, founded in 1949 by Mohammed Mosaddegh, aimed to distance Iran from Western influence and sought democratic reforms with constitutional governance and voting rights for the people. The party's formation came amid the oppressive Allied occupation of Iran during World War II, which led to the emergence of the Pan-Iranian School.

The Pan-Iranian School, initiated by five students, resisted foreign intervention and inspired nationalist youth to fight against the Allies' presence. When Mosaddegh spoke in parliament advocating for the nationalization of the oil industry, the Pan-Iranian students supported him and formed the National Front Party.

In 1951, Mosaddegh became Iran's prime minister and achieved the nationalization of the oil industry. However, internal conflicts persisted, leading to the formation of various national parties, including the People's Party of Iran, in opposition to the leftist Tudeh Party. The struggle against the Shah's regime continued, and in 1953, the Shah orchestrated a coup against Mosaddegh, but it failed. Afterward, the National Resistance Movement was formed, and my father, along with others, actively participated in its activities.

In 1961, when the environment became slightly more open, the second National Front was formed. However, the arrests and imprisonments of its members persisted, leading to the formation of the third National Front in 1966.

The fight for political and social freedom intensified in the late 1970s, with the demand for the correct implementation of the constitution and an end to political oppression. The fourth National Front Party emerged, representing the people's desire for true political freedom, alongside existing social freedom.

Then came the Iranian Revolution in 1979 and the establishment of the Islamic Republic of Iran, with Ayatollah Ruhollah Khomeini as supreme leader. However, the struggle for freedom and justice continued, as various factions vied for power and influence.

Throughout these challenging years, my father and other activists faced countless arrests and hardships as they fought for a better Iran. The story of the National Front Party and its fight for a democratic Iran remains an integral part of the nation's history, representing the human spirit's enduring capacity to persevere in the pursuit of justice and freedom.

As the Revolution was fomenting, the Shah attempted to mend tensions with the opposition. He offered to share power with them in the hope that it would stop the Revolution. He chose Shahpoor Baktiar to become the prime minister. Baktiar asked my father to join him in forming a new government, but my father declined. Instead, he chose ambassadorship to Spain in Madrid.

At this time, Iraq had invaded Iran, and the Iranian government was buying arms from anywhere they could find, one of which was the Israelis, channeled through Spain. My father was forced to sign a contract for the arms to be released to Iran. However, this contract was a scam by some Iranian individuals to steal money. The Iranian government was pressuring my father, saying that young Iranian soldiers were dying in the field and that he must sign the contract. My father, suspicious, didn't want to sign. The money ended up being stolen by representatives of the Iranian banks and government, and the arms were never delivered to Iran.

My father was asked to go to Iran for questioning, but he never even made it through Tehran International Airport. He just vanished. He simply vanished. It took my mother, uncles, and attorneys practically two years just to find out that he was alive and in prison. He was back in Evin prison, just as he had been under the Shah's regime. It took another two and a half years to get him out. In the end, it was determined that my father had done nothing wrong. We had known this all along, of course. He had just wanted to help his country and its people. In return, he had been humiliated, beaten, and tortured. But it didn't end there.

After he was proven innocent, the people who had stolen the money had fled Iran and my father was put under house arrest. He couldn't leave town, much less the country, for another 13 years.

I believe that my strength comes from my dad. He used

to tell me stories of those dark times in prison. Winters in Iran are cold and harsh. Half the country shares a border with Russia and Afghanistan. Tehran is a mile-high city, just like Denver, and it snows a lot in the wintertime. My dad told me that once a week, they would give him a break to walk in the prison courtyard, where there was a small pond with a fountain. He would strip off his clothes, break the ice, and enter the pond water. He would stare into the eyes of the soldiers standing on guard, cozy in their heavy uniforms and coats, holding their guns, watching him bathe in the freezing pond.

Almost all of my father's political friends had been executed after the Revolution. For those who had escaped the country, assassins were sent to behead them. My father said that he kept telling himself that he would not die in the prison because he had only one son, and that he would not die until he got to see his son one more time.

As I have already mentioned, he was tortured many times. His fingernails were pulled out. They sent electrical shocks to his groin. They played Russian roulette. All of this was to destroy him mentally. He said that if a prisoner was asked to "have supper with the warden," that person would never come back. When that happened, they would say goodbye to their cellmates, give them whatever they had left, and embrace them, because they knew they would never be returning to their cell. They did that to my father three times, except that every time, they would release him. Those actions took a psychological toll, but they never weakened him.

My father was eventually released from prison. On that day, they put a hood over his head and handcuffed his hands in front of him. He was escorted somewhere, but he had no idea where he was. He couldn't see anything. He could hear the boots of soldiers on the ground and the sounds of rifles being checked. They loaded him in the back of a truck, where soldiers sat around him. When he asked where he was being taken, they just told him to shut up, and not to ask questions. They drove for about 30 minutes. He was unsure of his fate, where they would take him, or what would happen when they got there.

The military truck came to a stop, and he was helped off the truck. He heard the soldiers' footsteps. He heard them check their guns. They took his hood off. Finally, he could see. The truck was stopped in the middle of nowhere, with about 12 soldiers. One of the soldiers turned my father, pointed him away, and told him to start walking. My father refused, saying, "If you are going to shoot me, do it so that I can look at your face."

The soldier pushed him hard. He almost fell. They ordered him to shut up and walk. And so he began to walk, leaving the soldiers and truck behind, expecting them to fire on him at any second.

The soldiers continued to play with their rifles, making noises as though they were about to shoot. Then all of sudden he heard footsteps, the engine turning, and the sound of the truck driving away.

He stood for a few minutes, wondering what was going on. Was it a trick? When he turned around, the truck was gone.

He walked a few miles until he flagged down a car and told the driver what had happened. That person was kind enough to give him a ride into town, and they gave him the equivalent of a few quarters for a pay phone. He called my mother to tell her that he was alive. My uncles picked him up and took him home, where he spent the next 13 years under house arrest.

Meanwhile, in the United States, I had become an American citizen and had applied for my mother, father, and sisters to join me. Ironically, their visas and green cards were sent to the American embassy in Madrid, Spain, waiting for my family to arrive there to interview for their applications. But my dad couldn't leave the country. My sisters, who lived in Spain and other parts of Europe, were able to come right away. Eventually, after 18 years of imprisonment and house arrest, my dad was allowed to come and visit me, leaving my mother and eldest sister, my sister's husband, and her children behind.

Within a month of his arrival in the U.S., my sister in Europe received a call from the Iranian government asking for my father. My sister relayed the message to my father. My father told me that he must go back.

"Hell no," I said.

After all these years of separation and what they had done to him, I couldn't bear for him to go back.

He told me that he must go, for the sake of my mother, my sister, and her family members that were still there. He told me that the government would send their bodies to us in bags to us if he didn't return.

It was a difficult time, because I was starting my training as a Boeing 737 captain at United Airlines. With a heavy heart, I said goodbye to my father. We didn't know what they would do to him. Kill him? Put him back in prison? Place back under house arrest? Thankfully, it was the latter. They'd told him that he could never again leave the country. However, we had made the decision that I would bring my sister, her kids, her husband, and my mother to the U.S., so if somehow my father got out again, he wouldn't have to worry about them.

It took about a year to get everybody out. Everybody,

that is, except for my dad. He was still being told that he could not leave. He was on a blacklist. He talked to his political friends who were still alive and asked them to find out why. Within a month, he was told that the government had opened his case from 19 years ago and that he was being targeted again.

That evening, the decision was made for him to leave the country, no matter what. They bribed people at the airport, and he was able to get out. Eventually, we were reunited back in the U.S. He resided with my mother in California and spent 25 wonderful years watching his children grow, get married, and have children of their own. He passed away on May 6, 2018.

My father, Ali Asghar Behnam, was the most democratic man I have ever known. On numerous occasions, he told me that he had forgiven his captors and everything they had done to him. The only crime that man ever committed was to love his country and his people. He endured so much and he remains an incredible inspiration to me and many others. More than 500 people showed up at his funeral. He meant so much to so many people.

Chapter 5

2018

My life and the people I love flash before my eyes: the time I left Iran, my mother, my sister, my kids being born and growing up, my father's illness. My father is in the last stages of his life. I tell myself that I will see him again. I will not leave him sick and alone.

Fly the aircraft, smooth and gentle.

Keep everything balanced, and don't overstress the aircraft, I tell myself. *Three hundred and eighty-one souls depend on it.*

The airplane rolls to the right in a 40-degree bank at a FL360 at Mach 0.83 (Mach 1 is the speed of sound). The instruments shake so hard that it's difficult to make out what they say.

The sound is deafening. It's as though a hundred-story

metal building is being crushed next to us in the cockpit.

I use the left aileron to try to level the plane and stop the roll, and the left rudder to compensate for the yaw.

I must be careful. An airplane at a 45-degree bank effectively weighs twice that of a plane flying straight and level. This is because such a steep bank imposes powerful gravitational forces, or g-forces, on the plane. In such a case, if you exceed the parameters of a normal flight, there's no guarantee she won't fall apart.

Shortly after 9/11, American Airlines Flight 578 hit wake turbulence, and the plane's first officer over kicked the rudders, creating a lateral force that snapped the vertical stabilizer—the vertical part of the tail—off the plane. They lost control and, tragically, the plane crashed, killing all 260 people on board and five on the ground.

I tell myself this will not happen. No matter how severe the problem is, I must focus. I must be gentle. After all, I'm essentially flying an out-of-control cruise missile at 550 miles per hour. There's no time for fear or panic. My focus is on keeping the blue side up—meaning, on the instrument panel's horizon indicator, I wanted to see blue (representing sky) on the top, and brown (representing ground) on the bottom. Keep the blue side up! Focus on flying the aircraft without autopilot and with minimal effort. It is like my car went full gas and my brakes gave out.

I take a deep breath and realize that I can still have control over the plane.

I make a decision.

Today will not be the day that we die.

I manage to level the plane and, now that I have my hands on the controls, I begin to realize that I will be able to fly, but it will be immensely difficult. That is an understatement. She's not behaving nor responding properly, and it's still too loud to talk at a normal level.

"What happened?" I yell to my copilot Paul.

"I don't know. The engine instruments are reading normal," he shouts back.

The instruments are lying to us.

"Maybe we had a midair collision?" offers Ed.

That's unlikely. Below 18,000 feet, there is plenty of air traffic, weekend warriors in Cessna 152s, and hundreds of other unidentified airplanes that aren't part of the system. But above 18,000 feet, where we are now, is completely controlled airspace. Everybody must be on an IFR (Instrument Flight Rules) flight plan. Traffic control must know exactly where everybody is. Plus, we have a traffic collision avoidance system, or TCAS, that will tell us if an intruder comes our way. But there isn't one. The TCAS is silent. At this altitude, at 36,000 feet, not even birds dare to fly.

"It doesn't make sense," I say, shouting through the cacophony.

After 35 seconds, the instruments on the right engine screen go blank. There is no oil quantity indication on the right side. All the gauges for the right engine are down.

"I think we have severe engine damage," I say. I hope that they can hear me over all the noise.

The drag is so extreme that I can't fly straight or maintain altitude.

I firewall the left engine—that is, I shove the throttle forward to max thrust.

I struggle to find a balance point.

I discover it instinctively, using every ounce of skill I've accumulated over 40 years of flying.

I ask Paul to perform a Severe Engine Damage Checklist. I have a full left aileron and a full left rudder to stop the roll. The airspeed drum is rolling backward.

I do not want to stall. You need speed to fly.

I lower the nose and vacate FL360.

By lowering the nose, I stabilize the airspeed from decreasing. Too slow, and the airplane simply will not fly. You fall out of the sky.

The cockpit is shaking so vigorously that Paul is unable to hit the Emergency Checklist (ECL) button. Ed helps Paul go through the checklist from memory—thank God for United's stringent pilot training—while I keep my hands on the yoke and throttle, performing a precarious balancing act between altitude and airspeed.

All three of us look at the right engine fire handle, and we confirm it. Paul pulls the fire handle, cutting off the fuel to the engine. The engine goes from runaway to dead. The initial vibration, on a scale of 1 to 10, was at a 15, but after we pulled the fire handle, it went down to a 7, and stayed like that until touchdown.

We're no longer within the bounds of the checklist. This last step wasn't on it. We're going above and beyond what we've trained and prepared for. We're creating new checklists in our heads, preparing ourselves to handle whatever the situation may bring.

The relief this moment brings is so brief it barely registers. The shaking has diminished but that statement is incredibly relative. The "7" still feels like in a 9.0 earthquake or like driving an 18-wheeler at 200 miles an hour over railroad tracks with no shock absorbers. It's extremely disturbing, highly chaotic, and entirely annoying. If it was just severe engine failure, shutting down the engine should have done it. Everything should be nice and smooth in the cockpit. But it's not.

In the aircraft simulator, when there's severe engine damage and you go through the checklist, you shut the engine down and you find yourself gliding through the air. It's smooth. But this is different. This is not business as usual. We should be able to talk. We shouldn't have to scream.

I continue to delegate while doing my best to keep the plane level.

I ask Ed to send out a mayday to Honolulu Control.

"Mayday! Mayday! Mayday! United Flight 1175. We've experienced severe engine damage. We are an emergency aircraft leaving flight level three six zero."

We need them to clear the airspace and give us priority.

There's silence.

What's likely only seconds feels like an eternity.

Finally, Honolulu Control answers. "Say again," as if they had never thought that a Triple Seven would declare an emergency over the open ocean, "How many souls on board, please?"

They ask because they need to be able to notify the authorities, the hospitals, the FBI, the police, firefighters, everyone that might need to be there should the worst happen, and we crash on the runway or miss the runway and ditch the plane in the water. Dead or alive, they need to account for everyone on board.

"Three hundred and eighty-one souls," Ed answers.

It's as if someone pours a bucket of ice water over me. Three hundred and eighty-one people. Fathers, mothers, kids, lovers, siblings—all their lives are in our hands. I tell myself that all these people have their trust in me. I cannot betray them.

"How much fuel, 1175?" Honolulu Control asks.

This is also a necessity. They need to know how far we can make it. We don't have enough fuel to change course. Unfortunately, this question isn't only about that. There's a more somber note to it. They also need to know what to expect should there be a crash landing. If we hit the ground on an empty tank that's one thing, but with a tank of gas, we're a cruise missile. Fifty thousand pounds of fuel at 600 miles per hour will vaporize anything.

"Fuel on board, one hour, 15 minutes," Ed replies.

❊ ❊ ❊

I ask for the next appropriate checklist.

Paul says, "Twenty-three thousand feet, airspeed 230 knots."

You need to know the airspeed to fly, and it's not possible to maintain altitude with one engine. We must keep the plane flying.

We begin our checklist, which tells you what altitude and airspeed you can maintain based on aircraft weight. Under normal conditions, we could maintain 36,000 feet with an airspeed of 265 knots. But with only one engine, there's no way we can maintain that.

We reduce airspeed toward 240 knots as we descend toward flight level 230 (23,000 feet).

As I reduce airspeed and start our descent, we enter the clouds at flight level 330 (33,000 feet). Visibility is zero. We're now in IMC Conditions (Instrument Meteorological Conditions). As we approach 240 knots, the aircraft starts to buffet and the stick shaker activates, indicating the onset of a stall.

To recover from a stall, you go max thrust and lower the nose. But I'm already at max thrust on the left engine, so I lower the nose to break the stall.

The aircraft descends at 3,000 to 4,000 feet per minute. I

can visualize that we're getting lower in a point in space, and the runway at Honolulu airport is rising. We're 200 miles out. If things continue this way, we won't make it to the airport.

※ ※ ※

I had been in a modestly similar situation before, at least regarding dealing with pulling up the nose. But not in a Triple Seven. I did this in a Mooney M20, which is a four-seat, propeller-driven plane. I was in South Lake Tahoe, flying with a student and two other passengers. I was teaching him how to take off, fly, and land in high-altitude environments. In Lake Tahoe, the elevation is over 5,000 feet above sea level, but on a warm day, the density altitude is almost 8,000 feet. That means that even when sitting on the ground, the airplane behaves as though it were at 8,000 feet. In other words, performance is worse on warm days. On that day, it would have been preferable to take off over the lake, but the wind direction made it so we had to take off toward a nearby mountain. We would then have to make a left turn and go downwind over the lake.

My student took to the air. His hands were at the controls. We were airborne, but the plane wasn't climbing as it should and the mountain was coming toward us. He got scared and started to pull the nose up.

 Chapter 5

"Don't pull the nose up," I quickly said.

"The mountains! The mountains!" was all he could say.

Some people think that when approaching a mountain if you keep pulling the nose up that everything is going to stop and be okay. Those people have seen too many movies. What will actually happen is the airplane will stop flying and stall. The plane will crash and you'll die.

As you increase the angle of the bank on the airplane, the weight of the aircraft and your body increases—at a 60-degree bank, the aircraft and your body weigh twice as much—and, at a higher airspeed, the aircraft stalls. This is called an accelerated stall, and when this happens physics begin to work against you.

The mountains were getting close.

We needed to make a shallow left turn.

My student was still scared. He was pulling and pushing the nose over. If he kept going at it that way, things weren't going to end well for either of us.

I quickly took control of the plane and put the airplane in a 10-degree bank.

If we'd gone to a 20- or 30- or 40-degree bank, we wouldn't have gotten as close to the mountain, but the weight of the airplane would have increased dramatically.

There would have been less lift, and we would have fallen out of the sky in an accelerated stall.

I pushed the screams of our passengers to the back of my mind and focused on relaxing and doing my job. I put the airplane in a shallow turn. We barely passed the tops of the trees. We continued out over a golf course, and I lowered the nose to build up airspeed.

In situations like these, airspeed and altitude are your friends. So many people in Lake Tahoe, and people flying out of other high-altitude airports, have died because they tried to fly as they do at sea level. They stall their airplanes, and they crash.

We continued out over the golf course and flew toward the airport to build up speed and climb. I contacted the airport on the radio and I told them that we had problems and that we couldn't climb. I requested permission to fly over the runway and to do a left 360 to gain altitude. They granted permission and shut the airport traffic down. We flew over the airport.

I lowered the nose within 50 feet of the runway.

I accelerated and built up airspeed.

I pulled the nose up and we began to climb higher and higher. We flew over the lake, circling up to 10,500 feet, and we crossed over the mountains.

I had saved the airplane and the three other people on board.

❊ ❊ ❊

But now I have 381 lives at stake.

I need to push the nose down to keep the plane flying, but if I push it down too much we will descend too rapidly and within 10 minutes we'll be at sea level.

That is not an option. We have 40 minutes to go. We need to glide as far as we can.

We are still in the clouds at 33,000 feet, and I have no outside visuals. I'm flying only with instruments. It's a matter of feeling and balance, like balancing rocks precariously on top of each other. I must remain focused on the task at hand.

This may seem like a strange comparison, but it's not. When balancing rocks, you must remain focused on what you're doing. If you think about the problems of the day, you won't be able to balance them. It's a form of meditation that I adore. After long flights, I love to go out by the river and balance some rocks. The sound of the burbling river and the chirping of birds and wind finding its way through the leaves of trees, combined with the required focus of placing river-worn stones on top of one another, is grounding and meditative. You're in the present and one with nature. I tell myself that I'll land the plane and balance rocks again. If one rock falls, it all collapses.

I remain calm and focus entirely on the task at hand. Three-hundred-and-eight one lives are in the balance.

Chapter 6

1972

Despite the struggles my family faced, I still had a lovely childhood that shaped me into the man I am today. When my father was not in prison or spending time with his family, he'd have his friends over to talk politics and poetry and of the bigger and better things that could be. I loved these talks, and from them I developed a hunger for knowledge and curiosity. Those evenings, I'd sit on his lap, the only kid among young adults between the ages of 25 and 30, and watch these large men with big mustaches talk of the future. These tremendous nights of intellect and joy shaped my world. I learned from these evenings the necessity of surrounding myself with those who know more than I do. My memories of these discussions would carry me through my youth and beyond.

Time would go on, and as I've mentioned, my father would

again find himself arrested by the Shah's SAVAK, the equivalent of the KGB, and put in prison. He never complained, and he avoided going into too much detail. He particularly took care to avoid discussing the darker parts.

It bears saying again that I grew up with an inspiring father who put his beliefs on the line, often before his family. He dared to speak out and challenge the status quo. He was courageous, maybe even to a fault, and watching him and my mother, and growing up in Iran during this pivotal and unstable time in history, taught me the importance of family, loyalty, hard work, integrity, and staying true to one's values. We were not wealthy by any means, but we enjoyed life. We loved one another and we loved our country.

My mother's life was peaceful when my father was not imprisoned. She spent her days doing housework, sewing, crafting, and embroidering pearls. Most of our family members came to Tehran, and we socialized with our relatives and their children. Tehran was very hot in the summers, and since my father didn't teach then, we'd go to Polour, on the Haraz River, for three months in the summers.

At first, we pitched tents there and we children played, climbed, and fished. These were glorious summers. When we got older, my father bought some land. He built a cottage and turned the land into an apple and apricot orchard, making it an even more beautiful place to spend the summers. The delicious fruit didn't hurt either.

※ ※ ※

Then there was the time I locked myself in a trunk. Notwithstanding the ongoing circumstances with my father, this was one of my early formative moments. I wanted to play hide-and-seek, but I had nobody to play with, so I decided to go ahead and hide anyway. Build a castle and they will come, I figured. Hide and they will seek. In my mind, I was probably fighting some invisible enemy, probably a cowboy or a bandit. But unfortunately, even then, that's not how the game is played.

I went to the back of this car to hide as part of my game, and I pulled the hood of the trunk down. It locked.

That wasn't good.

And it was not what I was expecting.

As one would expect, I became very scared and panicky. The car was something like 50 meters from my home. It was around two in the afternoon and most people were taking their afternoon naps. I was kicking and screaming and shouting, but no one could hear me. Each time I kicked at the trunk it would open a little more. I was a bit relieved. Maybe I wouldn't be trapped here after all. Perhaps I'd have a heroic escape story to recount.

I kicked again and the crack got larger.

A little more air. A little more light.

The air part was particularly good, because despite my heroic efforts, I was literally running out of air. The situation had changed, quickly, to one where I thought I was going to suffocate and die. I lost count of how many times I kicked that trunk. I began to give up. But I rallied. Giving up wouldn't solve anything. It never does. I was scared, but I wasn't crying. I did not lose myself. I always knew that if I kept doing something, eventually something would happen. Someone might hear a shout, or one of those kicks might finally break the lock and I'd be able to make my escape.

I kicked, I kicked, and finally, the lock gave out. I was free.

Now, unbeknownst to me, my mother had noticed that I was missing. She was looking for me, and when I finally got out, I came into the house and collapsed to the floor. I was sweaty and purple. I must have looked like I was dying. But I learned an important lesson that day. Even when the going gets tough, keep going—or you'll never get out of that trunk.

❊ ❊ ❊

Then there was the day I saw my future take to the air.

Once, when I was 9 and my father was out of prison, he took us all to Mehrabad International Airport in Tehran to see the planes take off and land. I already had the inkling of a passion for planes. I marveled at them, the tremendous sound, and the sheer engineering know-how that allowed humans the magic of flight. Whenever a plane would fly overhead, I'd gaze up, awestruck. But that day at the airport was the first time I'd ever seen one up close.

The sheer immensity of it enraptured me.

I was utterly spellbound as a Pan Am 747 took off into the air.

It was at that moment I knew I would fly that plane.

I ran and told my friends and family that I dreamed of becoming a pilot.

Everyone laughed. "Pilots? Those are gods," they told me. "Come down from the clouds." They told me that I wasn't good enough, that I'd never be good enough. But I didn't let it stop me.

If my father taught me anything, it's that you cannot let your detractors stop you. You must keep going and believe in yourself. I knew that deep down in my heart one day I'd realize my dream of becoming a pilot, even if there were times I didn't know *the how* of how I would achieve that dream. I held onto it my entire life. Why wouldn't I? Dreams are free, and I was obsessed. With any money I had from New Year's or birthdays, I'd buy model airplanes, put them together, paint them yellow, and write "Behnam Incorporated" in great big letters. I daydreamed of flying through the sky in a 747. While my friends would fly kites, I flew biplanes.

The obsession continued.

When I was 11, I went with my mom to visit her friend on the south side of town near an Air Force base. I could see the runway from her house, but it was the gliders that really caught my attention. A glider is quite simply a small plane without an engine. They're pulled down a runway by a cable attached to, in this case, a military truck, and once it reached the correct speed, the glider lifted off. At a few hundred feet, they released the cable, and you would just glide, smoothly, quietly, and majestically.

Seeing this, I pulled my mom's skirt, saying, "Please, please, please send me on this plane; send me on this plane!"

At first, she didn't care. It was expensive and money was hard to come by. But every month when we went to visit her friend, I'd go with her and, finally, after enough nagging, she gave in. I knew we didn't have much money, so her letting me go on the glider meant the world to me. The ride was phenomenal. I still smile just thinking about it. With no engine, it was blissfully quiet. Soaring on thermals, the glider climbed and turned, performing a ballet in the air. There was no anxiety, no airsickness, just total peace. In the air, I was free from worries and cares. I felt at home. All the world's troubles were left on the ground, and at that moment I had no doubt in my mind that I was meant to become an aviator. More than ever, I was convinced that my dream would come true. "This is it," I told myself. "I belong up here. I have absolutely no fear."

I was grinning ear to ear when I landed. I related my experience to my mother. She hugged me. She could see how happy I was. She told me that I was born to do great things, that I had a fire within me. And while she didn't say it then, she also knew that the odds would be against me. They were, and it didn't take long before this started to become apparent.

A few years later, my father would take me to go speak with the Iranian Air Force to ask about how I might become an airline pilot. It is a common path for pilots in Iran. You begin by working in the Air Force for six to eight years, and then, upon discharge, you go work for corporations or commercial airlines. When we asked, they asked me if I had a filling in my tooth.

I did, so I didn't qualify.

Of course, it had nothing to do with my filling. The Air Force was a job reserved for the elites, the sons of Shahs, the children of admirals and politicians. I was a nobody from a poor family with a father who opposed the Shah and was often in prison. There was no chance I'd become a pilot. But my father never discouraged me. He advised me, as he always did, to work hard.

And I did. I've worked hard from the moment my dream began back when I was 9. I'd just seen the Pan Am 747 take off. I knew that one day that would be me. I told my father that day at the Mehrabad Airport that I would make it happen. It may have seemed preposterous that a poor kid in Iran could ever achieve such a thing, but I was determined.

The engine roared as the 747 disappeared into the sky. My father looked at me and smiled.

Chapter 7

2018

I'm still in the clouds, still flying on instruments. There are no outside landmarks to guide my way. All I have to navigate with are those instruments, which, because of what's going on are themselves already of questionable reliability.

We must maintain a shallow descent rate of 1,200 feet per minute. I had already firewalled the left engine to max thrust, and it takes every bit of that power and my focus to keep descent at a steady and acceptable rate.

We continue the checklist.

Reading from the checklist, Paul says, "The best altitude is 23,000 feet and the airspeed of 240 knots. That's the best altitude and airspeed to fly the airplane, according to the Boeing 777 manual."

Reducing the airspeed causes the plane to buffet and shake even more than it already is. It's on the verge of stalling. Textbook solutions aren't going to work. The plane is so incredibly aerodynamically compromised, and the airflow over the right wing is so severely disrupted, that pushing the nose down to keep the airspeed up to keep the plane from stalling is not going to work. If we do that, we'd never stand a chance of making it to Honolulu. We're still 200 miles out from the runway. I go back to my most basic training: aviate, navigate, and communicate.

If you lose one engine on a two-engine aircraft, you don't just lose 50 percent power, you lose 80 percent. You lose symmetrical thrust. When all the power is coming from one engine, the aircraft is extremely difficult to handle. The right engine is inoperative but vibrating like crazy. Even though we have full power from the left engine, I realize that we can't fly at the book's airspeed, nor can I maintain the recommended altitude. I'm currently on what we call a CDAP (Constant Descent Angle Profile) to meet the earth, and hopefully the runway.

I keep looking at the engine instruments, trying to get as much information as I can.

There's no checklist for what is happening.

I calculate in my head my needed rate of descent for

what's needed to safely make it to Honolulu. I have 40 minutes to descend 36,000 feet, a controlled fall, a glide. Numbers don't lie. The airplane is disabled and it's struggling to maintain altitude. The left engine is pulling 90,000 pounds of thrust, with no thrust on the right side. It feels like I'm piloting a good plane on the left side, while dragging along a four-story building on the right wing. That's how much drag was created when the right engine cowling tore off.

I lower the nose, then bring it up, then lower the nose, and bring it up again, looking for the sweet spot. I find it between 245 and 255 knots. I keep it right there. It's like trying to balance a plate on my fingertips with a ball bearing in the middle for 40 minutes. The smallest amount of change can suddenly make the airplane uncontrollable.

Altitude. Airspeed. Distance.

Altitude. Airspeed. Distance.

Altitude. Airspeed. Distance.

I'm calculating the formula.

It repeats again and again in my head. *Altitude. Airspeed. Distance.*

"God please help me! Please take care of my passengers, crew, and aircraft," I say to myself quietly.

Altitude. Airspeed. Distance.

Altitude. Airspeed. Distance.

We've shut down and secured the engine and finished our checklists. I ask the chief purser to come into the cockpit and sit in the jump seat. She informs us that to no one's surprise, the passengers are quite alarmed. The aircraft was shaking violently. I'm very transparent and honest. I tell her what's happening, that we don't know the extent of the damage, that we shut one engine off. I tell her that we lost the right engine and that there's a distinct possibility that we may have to ditch the plane in the ocean. I tell her that I'll give her the signal to brace when we're about two minutes out.

She leaves.

I ask Ed to go back to the cabin and have a look at the right engine to better determine what we're dealing with.

He leaves.

I instruct Paul to get dispatch online, on SATCOM. Initially, someone else picks up, but they forward us to the appropriate dispatch sector for the flight. I still cannot take my hands off the yoke. I use the mic on the yoke to talk to dispatch. I tell them what's going on. They understand how bad the situation is.

Ed comes back with a short video of the right engine. It's oscillating, and the cowling is completely ripped off.

The airplane shakes violently, and I continue to focus.

Altitude. Airspeed. Distance.

Altitude. Airspeed. Distance.

Altitude. Airspeed. Distance.

Honolulu is still 150 miles away.

Chapter 8

1974

While I was born in Amol, I only spent three days there before we moved to Tehran, which is where I grew up. Every summer we'd go to Polour and then from there to Amol to see my grandma and grandpa. I loved the smells of the city. The smells of Amol, which is near the Caspian Sea, remind me of Seattle. It was very lush and green but also humid like Chicago or Washington, D.C. Lots of citrus trees provide plenty of oranges and tangerines and lemons to go around. The scent of fresh citrus in my grandmother's house still comes to mind. In those days, most roads were just dirt. When it rained, the smell of dust and rain and mud filled the air. A couple of very wide, large rivers wove through the valleys from the mountains to the Caspian Sea. These rivers were always full of fish.

Chapter 8

My mother, Azar Roshan, was born in November 1935 in Bandar-e-Gaz. Her father, Abbas Roshan, and her mother, Robabeh Roshan, were from Mazandaranand, born in Noor and Sari. Her parents had six children—four sons and two daughters. My mother was the fifth child and second daughter in the family. She spent her childhood in Bandar-e-Gaz. She has good memories from her childhood there. She lived in a big house with her grandparents on her father's side. Her grandfather was a businessman who traveled by ship from Bandar-e-Gaz to Russia for trade. When she was 5 years old, her family moved to Amol, where she lived with her grandparents in a large house overlooking the beautiful Haraz River. She spent her adolescence and educational days peacefully with her family in Amol. She had an interest in Persian poetry and literature, especially the work of Forough Farrokhzad. As a teenager, she often traveled with her mother to Sari to visit her relatives. She was 16 years old when her destiny changed during one of the trips to Bandar-e-Pahlavi, where she met her future mother-in-law.

My father—Ali Asghar Behnam—and his mother had moved to Bandar-e-Pahlavi. He was teaching there after having graduated from the University of Tehran with a bachelor's degree in chemistry. Azar and my father liked each other, and two years after meeting they got engaged in Amol. Two years after that they married and started living in Bandar-e-Pahlavi. They lived there for about four months until my father was transferred to Tehran, where they went, along with his mother and brother.

They lived in a rental house at first. Then they moved to a modest two-story home in Tehran. They had very happy days there. They had four daughters; I was their only son. My mother was a housewife who had a great interest in cooking and sewing. Over the years, she attended sewing workshops. She even got her diploma in sewing. She sewed our clothes as well as her mother's and grandmother's. She and my father, despite the hard times, gave us all a lovely childhood.

❊ ❊ ❊

During my childhood, as I briefly mentioned, my father had a property in the northern part of Iran in Mazandaran near the Caspian Sea. After years of vacationing in Polour, he purchased land in Takor, about 3 or 4 kilometers from the main village. My mother told me that when he first took her to their newly purchased property, she was beside herself. He'd purchased land without consulting her. My father promised he'd make it work. He promised her that he'd build a home there, and he did just that. He built a house on that land. It was beautiful, and we'd go there in the summers. He planted fruit trees and worked very hard to make the place what it became. Some of my fondest memories are from the times spent there in my youth. I remember going to the Haraz River and just sitting there watching the water, or at least what I could see of it. Early in the morning, you couldn't see anything, but as the land started to warm the fog would begin to lift. Eventually, it would separate from the river, and then, as if by magic, you'd suddenly see the other side. I loved this. It was a magical moment, and if my cousins were in town, I'd drag them along and take them with me to this perfect spot I'd found to watch the fog lift. And then we'd fish.

My dad and my uncle taught me how to fish. I quickly fell in love with fishing, and it's still something I do to this day. Once I knew how to fish, I'd get up in the morning, grab a fishing pole, and walk to the river.

I loved time outside to myself. I loved the peace and quiet and the smells of the early morning mist. I can still recall the dirt roads and humid air, my shoes sloshing through the mud on the way to the river. I'd walk through trees, weaving through the branches like a tiny adventurer, and feel the little drops of rain and mist on the leaves. I adored touching the tiny cool droplets of water, and I still do. Reaching the river, I'd sit and fish. It was wonderful, calm, and meditative.

Believe it or not, I'd catch hundreds of small fish. It was my way of providing for my family. I'd put them in empty burlap rice sacks, and I'd carry them back to our house, and my mom and my aunt would cook them for dinner. They'd be made into fish fries. My family and our neighbors would enjoy hundreds of these little fried fish. They were small but absolutely delicious. I still love to feed my family, and if I ever have extra fish, I'll usually give some to my friends.

While I enjoyed fishing alone, fishing with my dad and uncle was even better. My uncle and I once caught the biggest rainbow trout that either of us had ever seen in one of those rivers near Takor. We didn't do it with fancy gear. He used a 15- or 16-foot bamboo rod. We connected a line to the top of the rod and a spinner at the end of the line, so when you threw the rod over to cast, the rod would be 15 feet away from you. It was about 15 or 16 feet of line going down to the river, and you'd move the rod against the flow of water to get the spinner to spin for the fly. Believe it or not, with that rainbow trout, we ended up setting the record for the Persian version of *Field & Stream* at that time. We even made the cover.

There were so many fish in those days. My dad had a Jeep Willys, as they did in the TV series *M*A*S*H*, that had storage under the seats that we'd fill up with fish to bring to the neighborhood camp and share with the families there. Between the three of us, we were looking at 200 or 300 fish every day. We caught all sorts of fish, but I especially loved catching wild rainbow trout. It is still my favorite fish to catch.

❇ ❇ ❇

There were other times in the countryside when I was a bit mischievous. It wasn't just me; there were other children there as well. We were always playful—and sometimes, destructive. We'd hit sparrows, and catch and cut off the lizards' tails, and then laugh. Our parents would tell us to stop, to not abuse those creatures of God, but we thought we knew better. We didn't. We were kids, and I was always pushing the boundaries.

When I was 4, I once went off to play hide-and-seek with my older cousin. I went to the backyard to hide. There was a small pool back there about a meter in size, full of dirty water and moss. Unfortunately, in my rush to hide, I slipped and fell in. Thankfully for me, my cousin, who was 6 at the time, was there and he grabbed my back and brought me out of the small pool. They dumped cold water on me afterward to clean me off, which wasn't the best feeling. I was freezing. This wouldn't be the last time I'd have a run-in with water during these family vacations.

One Friday when I was 5, we set up a tent on our land and we had some guests over. People used to bring horses to ride on Fridays. I went and hit the back of one of the horses with my hand. Not surprisingly in retrospect, the horse didn't like this much. It decided to let me know and it kicked back and hit me in the face with its hoof. My lips were torn open, and I lost four teeth. My head swelled up to the size of a pillow. I gave my mother quite a scare. But I recovered. Thankfully, they were just baby teeth.

There was also the time in Polour when I found a baby eagle. It had just left its nest and it couldn't fly. It was running and trying to flap its wings, but it was either too weak or it couldn't figure it out. It was exhausted, and it just gave up. I went to it, and it looked me in the eyes. The eagle didn't try to fight me. It was as if he wanted me to rescue him. We looked at each other for a little while and, once I felt it was safe, I reached out my hands slowly and grabbed it. I held the baby eagle against my chest, comforted the injured bird, and brought it back to the camp where my family was staying.

I told my mother that I'd found this baby eagle and that I wanted to keep him. It was a dark brown that was made even more brilliant in the sun. My parents told me that keeping a baby was a big responsibility. I didn't believe them then, but as an adult now, I recognize that they were right. But in all their incredible patience and kindness, they let me keep it on the condition that I would have to take care of it and feed it. They made it very clear that eagles eat meat and stuff like that. But the first thing that we'd need was a cage to keep him safe from predators. My dad, my uncle, and I decided to make one. We had some chicken wire and I collected a few sticks. Together, we assembled a cage. It was rickety, but it did the job well enough. Honestly, it was just okay, but it was nice in that the eagle was visible. It was a crafty little cage. It was my eagle's home. Next I needed to tend to my winged friend's food.

We were still in our vacation spot in Polour. and we had a limited amount of food. My father would go shop for food at the end of each week, but this eagle was a ferocious eater, and my mother didn't want it fed with our food. This is where my trusty slingshot came in. I didn't need trips to the store; I could hunt for my eagle's food. So I got to practicing. I was determined to get really good at it. After all, I had an eagle to feed. Pretty soon, I was able to take out birds and lizards and mice and gophers and the like with pretty good accuracy. I'd bring them to my eagle. He seemed happy with the spoils from my hunt. I'd take him out of the cage and hold him to my chest and massage and feed him. He was my friend. I kept my eagle all that summer in Polour. The two of us shared two wonderful months in the countryside, and when we went back to Tehran at the end of the summer, I took my eagle with me. He rode along with me in the back seat of the car.

Back in Tehran, the next task was to figure out what to do with the baby eagle. We placed his cage by the swimming pool in the backyard. It was adorable watching him awkwardly walk around the pool. He was growing like crazy. He knew my footsteps and the sound of my voice, and he knew when it was lunchtime and dinnertime. I no longer hunted for his meals. I just fed him raw meat or chicken, and he loved it.

Our friends and family came and visited the eagle. Why wouldn't they? There was an eagle in our backyard who loved having an audience. He'd sit right at the edge of the pool and spread his wings, the span of which was almost six or seven feet. It was a sight to behold.

One day my mother told me that there'd been a lot of eagles hanging around, just hovering and circling around our part of town. It seemed like they were circling over our house, but they weren't. My baby eagle would look up, spread his wings open, and just keep looking up as the other eagles flew overhead. I knew that sooner or later he'd take to the sky again and be free. I wanted that for him. I wanted him to be with his friends, but at the same time, I knew it was going to make me very sad. One day when I returned from school, the eagle was gone. He was back in the sky, flying and soaring along the wind currents on his majestic wings.

Just like that, my eagle was gone.

Chapter 9

2018

With the cowling on the engine gone, it's obvious what's impacting the aerodynamics. Without a cowling—the outer covering of the engine—the engine is exposed directly to the elements, and airflow is drastically uneven. There's a strong risk of the aircraft breaking apart, and the aerodynamics of the airplane render it extremely difficult to fly. The wing shakes as violently as the plane. It's clear: We are in a compromised jet over the Pacific Ocean. We have no visual references. We are in the clouds aviating on instruments alone.

I continue to focus on flying while Ed and Paul work through various checklists. We can't engage the autopilot nor the autothrottle. I have to hand-fly the aircraft and keep everything smooth. The important thing for me, in my mind, is to maintain positive control of the jet.

I am completely zoned in. We have to focus our minds and keep things set on sorting out a safe landing for this plane. That is the most important thing—not only to land, but also to land as smoothly as possible.

We are pretty sure the weather is still looking good in Honolulu. Paul is based in Washington, D.C. (out of Dulles International), and wanted to fly to Honolulu, so he had bid for TDW (Temporary Duty) in San Francisco to fly to SFO. This was his third trip to Honolulu. I'd been flying to Honolulu for over 30 years. I mostly fly Honolulu to Guam or Honolulu to Denver flights. Thankfully, we're all very comfortable with its airport. Ed is actually from Honolulu, and he's flown for the Coast Guard out of Oahu.

When you lose an engine, you have to determine the most suitable airport for a potential emergency landing. Together we decide that our destination, Honolulu, is the best airport for us because of our familiarity with it, the environment, the terrain, and the availability of emergency equipment and services.

I visualize it in my mind.

I can see it.

I can see us approaching the runway and landing smoothly and safely.

The plane shakes tremendously.

I keep my focus.

Altitude. Airspeed. Distance.

I keep the plane stable. It takes every ounce of my strength and energy to balance the chaos of the situation.

Altitude. Airspeed. Distance.

I'd already turned direct to Honolulu to cut the distance and time by almost seven minutes. (The official airway and procedures are never perfectly direct.) HCF, Honolulu control, hands us over to Honolulu tower. They tell us to contact Honolulu tower at 118.3. Paul does just that, and he asks them to make sure they have emergency equipment standing by.

The tower confirms the equipment is ready.

They report that we should aim for runway 4R.

"We're unable to," I say. "It's too short for our configuration with an engine out. We'd like to go to 8R. It's longer."

Air traffic control gives us a couple of level-off altitudes, but I tell the guys to tell ATC that we're unable to level off. They wanted us to follow the normal descent profile—a series of step-downs. I keep asking for the lower altitude. I need to maintain constant descent angle. I'm so focused on the instruments that things, on and off, appear in slow motion.

I can't break focus, even for an instant. The shaking is so violent. At one point, I wonder if the entire plane is going to break into pieces.

I ask Ed to change the vectors to something closer to the land. If we have to put the plane down in the water, the water closer to the land will be calmer.

We continue our descent. Paul finishes our approach descent checklist. I ask the guys to make sure that everything on the checklist is complete.

Altitude. Airspeed. Distance.

Even though I'd already seen the video of the damaged engine, my brain is telling me something else is going on. I have Ed go back out of the cockpit a second time to check on the horizontal stabilizer, to see if everything is all right. The plane is just not doing what it is supposed to do. The number of variables seems to keep growing. It seems that losing 36,000 feet of altitude was too big a goal to achieve. So I focus on losing a thousand feet per minute.

Altitude. Airspeed. Distance.

I keep the mantra going in my head, constantly checking the numbers.

Altitude. Airspeed. Distance.

Ed comes back and tells me that he went to midship and saw that the back was shaking violently to the point of being hard to see. We have babies, kids, young adults, elderly, and handicapped passengers. I saw them before the flight. I'm piloting with a small village on board. Travelers to Hawaii are normally going there for vacation or to get married. It's the day before Valentine's Day.

We keep going.

We keep descending.

We keep our focus on the task at hand. The passengers' lives are literally in our hands. Eternity is a breath away, and there is nothing but ocean beneath us.

Altitude. Airspeed. Distance.

As we come upon our final approach, Paul says that there is a go-around procedure at this airport for single engines due to the high terrain at the end of the runway. But today, I decide that a go-around is not an option. I have full thrust on the engine to keep the airplane flying with a shallow rate of descent in a clean configuration. I don't think that the aircraft will be able to go around with the gear and flaps down. We're just going to have to land. And we have only one shot.

Altitude. Airspeed. Distance.

Honolulu control gives us our vectors for downwind and I ask the guys to help me see the runway. Air traffic control tells us to level at 10,000 feet. I tell Paul that we can't level off and maintain altitude because even with full power applied to the left engine, we're still descending. We can't maintain altitude. If we were to follow normal procedure, we might not make it to the airport. All I can do is focus on the instruments.

Twice, the airplane nearly got away from me at 33,000 feet. A stall at this lower altitude would be disastrous. I ask God again to protect the passengers and crew and to help us land safely.

We have no runway options. Runway 4R is too short; 8L is long enough, but it is closed that day. We have no choice. We have to shoot a nonprecision RNAV approach to runway 8R, hand-flown, in IMC conditions. This is very challenging, on top of the emergency we have been dealing with for the past 40 minutes.

At 10,000 feet, Ed reaches over and puts my shoulder harness on. I can't even pause to do that by myself.

Altitude. Airspeed. Distance.

Two minutes out, the flight attendants tell the passengers to brace for landing.

Come on. Come on. Come on. Just a thousand more feet. Stay together for me. Stay together for me.

I tell the guys in the cockpit that I'm not sure how the airplane is going to behave as we start putting the flaps and slats out to slow down. Normally, the last 10 to 15 seconds are crucial to the safety of the flight, but I have no idea how much damage was done to the wing.

I tell them that I'm going to come in high and fast, using a CDAP (Constant Descent Angle Procedure) teardrop approach.

All my focus is on landing this plane on the runway.

We start lowering the flaps. Flaps 1 lower when we're at 240 knots. They come down just fine.

I ask for gear down, and we receive a green light.

At 1,000 feet, I ask for Flaps 5 and reduce airspeed to 200 knots.

At 500 feet, Paul tells the passengers and flight crew to brace, brace, brace.

At 200 feet, I ask for Flaps 20 and reduce airspeed to 180 knots.

We touch down at that speed and, with God's grace, we land just fine.

It's one of my best landings ever. It was as if my hands

had become an extension of the wings, and my feet were the landing gear. The guys in the cockpit and the passengers on the plane would later tell me that when the aircraft landed, they didn't feel a thing.

Chapter 10

1972

It was another beautiful summer in the mountains. Tehran had serious smog issues. So during the summers, the mountains, with their fresh, invigorating air, were our escape.

Near the bottom of our summer property was a massive river that was maybe 400 or 500 feet across. Sometimes the water was rough and crazy, and other times it was soft and smooth. We'd play by the water, cross the river, and climb the nearby mountain. Some days my mother would send us up the mountain with a purpose. We were given burlap sacks and told to climb the mountain and get some snow, which we would use to keep food cold. When my mother was a child, she and her family had it even worse when it came to refrigeration. For her, the meat was placed in a cool crypt or a basement. It was

20 steps down to where the meat was hung from the basement ceiling, wrapped in cloth to keep out insects and flies.

On these glorious mornings, we set out at around seven in the morning, walking sticks in hand, and hiked our way to the snow. The distance depended on what kind of winter we'd had. We either had to hike up a long way to get some snow or, if it'd been a particularly bad winter, the base of the mountain would do. On the occasion of this story, it took about five hours to get to the snow. When we reached it, we used a pot I brought for a shovel, and we scooped and packed the snow into our burlap sacks. We tied the filled bags to our walking sticks and hoisted them up across our shoulders, looking like scarecrows climbing down the hill. We'd fall and stumble. Sometimes we'd roll up the bags and push them down the hill, running after them. We finally got back around six or seven in the evening, at which point some of the bags had turned to water.

Back at the house, my mother took the remaining bags of snow, and with them she made us delicious, fresh ice cream. It was the best ice cream in the world, handcrafted in the middle of nowhere by my mother. She used a large bowl and a smaller pot. She put the surviving snow in the bowl, the ingredients in the pot, and then the pot in the bowl. Then with the pot's handle, she stirred and stirred and stirred and stirred clockwise by hand. Sometimes it took a whole hour for it to get cold enough to become ice cream. Often it was vanilla, but sometimes she put a delicious sour cherry syrup in. Regardless of the flavor, once it was ready, we had to rush and eat it before it melted.

There were other adventures. We played hide-and-go-seek in the dark. One night, running around outside the house, my cousin fell into a six-foot hole my dad had dug for an outhouse. He was just running and then suddenly disappeared. It was hilarious. No one was hurt, and thankfully for my friend, the outhouse had yet to be christened. The homes in the area we stayed in were all situated in a sort of line. Their roofs were made of clay tops, and one day we had the bright idea to sneak over and crawl on top, pulling ourselves forward like commandos to spy on our neighbors. We were curious—and it didn't hurt that they had seven daughters.

At age 12, we weren't allowed to mingle or chat with girls. We'd seen them at a wedding and had wanted to see them again. But one of us was making too much noise. We were caught. They started screaming that someone was on the roof, and we ran across the clay roofs back to our home, except for my cousin, the same one who fell into the outhouse hole. He had disappeared. We kept running until we realized that we were missing one of our team.

He had fallen through a ventilation hole in the middle of the roof—luckily landing onto some hay in a stable with cows and chickens. We climbed down and doubled back to the house with the stable, knocked on their door, and did our best to explain the situation. With a bit of luck, we managed to save him.

※ ※ ※

The first time I nearly died I was 11. A flood had come through and the river was high. I was with three other friends. They were more city boys than I was. I had a bit of an advantage out there in the mountains. One, however, was a wrestler. He was bigger than the rest of us, so we made him carry all our things. We'd set out that day to hunt quail with BB guns for my mother to prepare for dinner. The river was turbulent and ran with a vengeance. It would be difficult to cross. There was a bridge a few miles up from where we were, but that was a long walk and a particularly less exciting journey. We weren't *not* going to cross. How hard could it be? I was confident. I was a strong swimmer and had no worries or fear. Fear has never been something that I felt. I can see how something might be dangerous, but I've always taken it in stride. I have a tremendous desire for adventure. I'm fueled by the idea of sticking my head around the corner to see what is there—to push the envelope and take the risk. So by the riverside, I had a noble idea. We were going to get to the other side. But *how* we were to get across was wherein I laid my plan. Since the water was rougher than usual, I decided we'd use a rope to cross. I'd walk upstream, tie it off on our side of the bank, and jump in and swim to the other side where I'd tie the rope to a tree, and then, like commandos, we'd all simply make our way across. It was because of ideas like this, my mom told me, that if I'd been in Iran after the revolution when Iraq and Iran went to war, not only would I have killed myself, but I would also have taken all my friends with me.

I walked upriver a few hundred yards to where the water was calmer and secured the rope around a large rock, tying the other end around my waist. I double-checked the knot and jumped in.

It wasn't easy. The water was powerful, and I struggled against the current, but I made it to the other side. Untying the rope from my waist, I secured it on a tree and signaled to my friends to cross. The first two joined me on the other side. It wasn't easy for them either, but they managed. The third to cross was my cousin, who was a bit smaller than the rest of us. As he crossed, he grew tired, his hands slipped, and he fell into the raging waters and was swept away downstream.

I dove right in.

I couldn't bear to lose him. I didn't even pause to think

about what could happen—the consequences my friends on shore would have to face, going up and telling his parents and my parents that their sons were dead. That was of no mind to me. I couldn't worry. I had no time to spare. I had to save my friend's life.

The river that so swiftly pulled him downstream pulled me after him as well. I struggled through the rapids, caught up, and managed to get hold of him.

The water continued to sweep us away.

We were knocked about, smashed up against rocks like rag dolls tumbling down the river. I hung onto my cousin for our dear lives. My head bobbed above the surface. I spotted a branch near the side of the water and furiously swam toward it and helped my cousin grab on and climb up. He made it and stood on a rock, but I wasn't able to. I was too exhausted and too weak. I slipped into the river and was swept away, smashed about between stones and rocks. I covered my head with my arms to protect it.

About a mile down the river, the water finally smoothed out and the river widened. Totally spent, I just managed to make it to the shore. I pulled myself out and lay there, exhausted, trying to catch my breath.

I had survived.

My friends ran alongside the river and down the hills to

try to catch up to me and help as I was swept further and further downstream. They later told me they'd spent some of the time panicking and worrying about what to tell my parents if they found my dead body. They'd assumed I was dead, and they were as relieved as I was to find me alive, though beaten up and bloody.

I was able to save my cousin, but I almost lost my own life as a result. I was grateful to be alive. Thoughts had rushed through my head as I was flung down the river. I was helpless. I had no control over the situation. All I could do was pray that I'd be okay.

We went home that day birdless and shaken. Of course, it wasn't long before the story broke. Everyone talked about it, how two of us had almost died. My mom admonished me a little bit—she wouldn't be doing her job otherwise—and she told my friends to be careful if they kept following me around on my adventures. There were no hospitals nearby, so it was dangerous for us to get hurt. I got an earful from my parents, but they also knew that I wasn't the kind of kid who was going to sit back and be a spectator. I wanted to go out there and have a major role to play in this theater of life. I think this is where an aspect of my leadership comes from. From a young age, people loved to be around me. Our days would be full of adventure. Nothing was going to be just "normal." Every day had to be something different, whether it was chasing quails, fording rivers, or trekking up mountains for snow. If I heard about a bear or mountain lion, I wanted to go track it down. What would we do if we found it? We'd worry about that later.

Such adventures seem to happen less often these days. Back then there were no smartphones or the internet. We had to go outside and make something of our days. It was like this for the whole family. It's not like camping at Lake Tahoe as I do now, with an RV. With an RV in Tahoe, we don't have to worry about food or cooking. We plan out our days, be it fishing or hiking or boating. But during these summers in Iran, once we were there, we'd help our parents unpack, and then the day would be ours. We would make of it what we would.

The next day after the river incident, we went back and the rope was still there. I tied my cousin to myself to prevent the previous day's scenario and we stepped into the river. We safely crossed, and that night my mother made us all a delicious dinner: quail.

Chapter 11

2018

After touchdown, we exit on taxiway RG, and I bring the airplane to a stop.

Paul taps me on the shoulder. "You can let go now, Captain. You can let go."

It takes a moment to hit me. We'd landed. We made it.

My right hand is still on the left throttle, and my left hand is practically glued to the yoke.

For the past 40 minutes Paul had been watching me, wondering when my body was going to give up. But it didn't, and neither did I.

I'm completely drained, yet focused. I want to find a bed and just sleep. But there's no time for that yet.

The fire marshals and rescue crews stand by. They were there before we landed. It's good that they are there, but there's still a disconcerting feeling in my stomach from their presence. They remind me of what could have happened and the lives that could have been lost.

We're still not sure what caused the problem in the first place. We keep the left engine running. I don't want to risk anything, and they still need to check on the right engine to see if smoke or fire is present.

We wait as they check it.

Finally we get the go-ahead. No smoke. No fire. It's a relief.

There is, however, hydraulic fuel leaking. That's not ideal, but they tell us it's safe to taxi the airplane to the gate and to shut the engine down.

We do just that.

At the gate, I remain in my seat, my hands still holding the controls.

I hear cheers from behind me. The passengers, whose lives were literally in my hands, can now finally relax. But we're not done. We still have duties to attend to, the first of which is those cheering passengers. They had just experienced something horrific. I turn to the guys in the cockpit. "Let's go and stand by the exit door and thank the passengers."

We step out of the cockpit. The passengers are relieved

but visibly shaken. People are crying and hugging. Some call their families. The cabin is a mess. Things are knocked around. Clothing and suitcases strewn about.

We stand by the door and shake everyone's hand as they step off the plane. They tell us how they thought they'd never see their loved ones again. Someone takes a picture. We shake more hands. There are men trying to be tough. Others are in tears. A little girl with blonde hair in pigtails walks down the aisle toward me. She must be only 4 or 5 years old. I can only imagine how hard it was for her. It reminds me of how precious, yet fragile, life is.

My thoughts go back to my son, Alexander. My now ex-wife and I almost lost him when he was born. We weren't even sure he'd make it past 72 hours. He was only six and a half pounds when he was born and within three days, he'd lost nearly a pound. We weren't sure what was wrong. He was unable to process food. He took in milk, but nothing came out. It was terrifying. Nothing was going through his system, and we worried we would lose him. We brought him to the emergency room, and it was lucky we did. They immediately took him in for surgery and as they operated on our newborn son, Beth and I held our breath, praying that he would be okay. Later they told us that if they hadn't operated immediately, he would have died. The problem, they discovered, was with his intestines. The sac around them had not properly formed and his intestines had grown outside the sac and gotten twisted. Thankfully, the surgeons were able to untwist them, and Alexander survived. The recovery, however, wasn't immediate. Our son was in a coma for six days. I never left the hospital that whole time. I sat beside my son and visualized his future and the life that we'd share. I visualized him healthy and athletic. I imagined his graduations, falling in love, his first job, his first heartbreak. I could see him all grown up. He'd be six feet seven inches tall, I thought (which he is), and 225 pounds. (which he also is). I prayed and prayed and prayed. I brought him baseball gloves and a football. He would survive and they would be his. I visualized the fishing trips and sailing adventures that we would go on. We'd go running. I was going to teach him how to tie his shoes and how to ride a bike. I'd fix his tie before prom. Those six days, those 144 hours, were some of the hardest days of my life, but I never gave up my faith. I never gave up my belief in the communion I have with a Greater Power.

One day, while waiting for him to recover, I took a walk in the parking lot. It was a cloudy day, but I needed some fresh air. My wife kept watch on Alexander, but I didn't want to go far from his side. As I walked, I broke down crying. It was all too much. I asked God to take my life so that my son could live. And as corny as it may sound, I kid you not, the clouds separated, and the warmth of the sun struck my skin. It was such a healing and powerful moment. I took it as a sign that everything was going to be okay. I went back inside and told my wife that I knew as much. A day later, our son opened his eyes.

That moment flashes through my mind as I watch the young girl with pigtails walk toward me down the aisle. She comes up to me and says with a big smile, "That was cool!" I can't help but grin. She tells me it was the best roller-coaster ride ever. I'm still smiling as I watch her leave, but on the inside I'm like a volcano. I'm doing my best to hold it together.

A lady with an Australian accent tells me that it was the best landing ever. I hold a baby and think of the fragility of life, and again, my son. All the things I'd visualized and prayed for about my son had become a reality. He became an athlete, and a good one at that, earning a scholarship as a swimmer to Cal Poly San Luis Obispo. He graduated and got into medical school, where he is now. He's a strong, handsome young man. I can't help but become emotional holding that baby on the plane. That child has their whole life ahead of them, and for the past 40 minutes that baby's life was in my hands. I was honored that I could make a difference in that mother and child's life. I give her back her baby and tell her just that.

A few others thank me, and suddenly the passengers are all gone.

I gather up the flight attendants. We hug them and I thank them for jobs well done. I take a moment to myself to thank the Creator and the airplane for getting us down safely.

We disembark and go down to look at the damage.

The cowling, the cover around the engine, is, as we suspected, completely ripped off. Despite the beauty of an engine's engineering, it's not something you ever want to see on a plane that you're flying, and here we were with the engine completely revealed. Seeing the damage, it's no surprise there was so much drag. We were lucky none of the debris hit the tail. If a piece, even a tiny one—after all, 10 pounds at 500 miles per hour exerts around 5,000 pounds of force per square inch—had struck the plane, it could have severely damaged the tail, or even taken it off completely. And you can't fly an airplane without a tail, even if you were Chuck Yeager or Neil Armstrong. If that had happened, the plane would have rolled, and we would all have died.

The maintenance personnel mill about, seeing to various things. Upon closer inspection, it seems as though some of the fan blades had torn loose and hit the fuselage. Thankfully, they struck the stringer, which is sort of like a rib. It's an incredibly strong part of the plane. If they had hit elsewhere, they could have ripped a hole in the fuselage, pressurization would have been lost, and we would have had to rapidly descend to 10,000 feet, per the aircraft's manual. The plane might not have made it.

We take a lot of pictures and some videos. Someone snaps a photo of Paul, Ed, and me.

My phone has been ringing this whole time. People have been trying to reach me since they learned the plane was in distress. United keeps calling. They want to speak with the captain to learn what happened. A United van picks us up and takes us to a United Airlines operations facility. Partway there, we're rerouted. News agencies are crowding the terminal, so we go down the ramp where luggage is sent. They take us to the United headquarters at the airport, where they'd cleared a conference room for us. It's empty but for Ed, Paul, me, and the station manager. I text my girlfriend and my kids to let them know that everything is okay and not to worry, even if they hear anything on the news.

The station manager asks us if we need anything.

We don't. All we need is a phone and a quiet room. We thank him, and he leaves us. Paul, Ed, and I are finally alone, finally facing the immensity of what we'd all survived.

Chapter 12

1975

.This is not something I recommend you try

I was teetering on the edge of a cliff. Earlier that day, I'd gotten the key to my father's Jeep without my parent's knowledge. I didn't have a driver's license, but I knew how to drive. I'd gotten my sisters and cousins and our housekeeper's children—five kids in total—in the back of the mint green Jeep Willys to go into the village to get some gum and candies. We were in the hills outside of Takor where my family had a property. These were beautiful dirt roads that wound about like those in Lake Tahoe. As we headed home, we had some fun driving. When we went up a hill, I'd step on the gas, quickly turn the wheel, and skid around the corner. It was a blast. Everyone loved it. They'd cheer me on and dare me to do it again. It was a glorious time. Until it wasn't. As we approached a bend, I turned left. The back of the car started to slide. I heard a scream from one of the kids in the back. I took my eyes off the road for a second and turned to look toward the backseat. The back door had opened and one of my cousins had fallen out of the car. I turned forward again. We were going to go over a cliff. I slammed on the brakes, but the car slid. We'd gone off the road and were headed over the cliff.

The drop was almost a thousand feet.

Mercifully, the truck stopped. It rested on one rock. We teetered, balanced between life and death, between heaven and Earth. The only thing that would keep us from eternity was a miracle.

I immediately turned off the engine.

The Jeep sat there, wobbling slightly. It was silent except for the gentle rocking of the car's body against stone. I wanted everybody to get out quickly, but any sudden move, any shift of weight, might send the car over the edge. I knew neither the conditions at the front of the car, nor by how much of a thread we were hanging. All I knew was that we were in trouble.

Someone carefully and slowly opened the back door. The car wobbled a bit, then steadied. One by one, as each kid got out, the rest of us held our breath. All I could think about was my responsibility for these kids, my family. Their lives were in my hands.

After all the kids got out, it was my turn. I looked back. The door was still open. I jumped to the back seat and ran out of the car. We'd all made it. The car was still balancing on the edge of eternity. We dusted ourselves off and walked down the hill to find my cousin who'd fallen out of the car. He was covered with dirt and a little scraped up, but otherwise fine.

Still shaken, we walked quickly down the hill to my parents' house. We were silent, still in shock from what had happened.

By this time, most people nearby had heard the horrendous noise that echoed in the mountain when the car ran up on the rock. My dad knew something bad had happened, but they couldn't see us because we were about a mile away. Nonetheless, he knew. He'd already gathered my uncles and his friends and their cars to drive up and see what had happened. They came across us as we were walking down the hill. They made sure that we were okay. I told my father that everyone was all right, and I went back with them to the car, which was still resting on a small boulder. They tied ropes to it and with all three cars pulling fast, they managed to bring it back onto the main road.

Death was denied another day, but that wasn't the end of it. I sure got a talking-to. Now, neither my dad nor my mom ever hit us. In circumstances like these, my mother would just smirk, even though she likely wanted to say something like, "You shouldn't be doing something like that." I could tell that part of her was happy that I was willing to push the envelope. As an adult, when I take my parents flying or sailing on a fast-powered boat, my mom loves it, though my dad is a bit more conservative and doesn't show it as much.

My father sat me down after the incident with the Jeep. He was glad we were safe, but he told me it was a dumb thing to have done. What was I thinking? What did I think the result would have been if we weren't so lucky? But he knew the reason. It was stupid and it was silly. He knew that as I got older, he would have to guide me. I was the only son among four sisters, and they didn't do anything like this. I was not a normal boy. I always pushed the envelope. I always did things that were daring and dangerous and crazy, though not without calculation—even if at times, as with the car, the situation spiraled out of control. He asked me what I would have done if my sister or cousin died and that I'd been responsible. He asked me how I'd carry that weight for the rest of my life.

I looked into my father's eyes. I knew the toll his prison time took on my mother. I'd seen it in her eyes as well. I questioned what my destiny would be and how it would be linked to him. Looking into his eyes on that day ignited something within me. At times, life would cause this flame to dwindle to embers, but it would never be extinguished. It would grow again, stronger than before. My father taught me to never give up. Thoughts and fears frequently vanquish our courage and our confidence. But if we allow that capitulation, we seal our fate. We don't often analyze these situations as they happen. In the immediate aftermath, we're just grateful to be alive. But in my heart, deep down in my soul, I knew that I'd survived for a reason. I had a destiny to fulfill. As pilots, we're trained to keep our emotions in check, to be analytical, to trust in science. And in my case, in divine providence. After all, it has seen me through so much.

Chapter 13

2018

The station manager leaves Paul, Ed, and me, and we take a moment to congratulate each other. We're shaken, but I feel that as the captain, I need to keep it together. I ask them for their thoughts. We have nothing to hide. We go over what happened. The next step is to follow the ALPA protocol. In cases such as these, ALPA acts as an intermediary between pilots and airlines.

ALPA, or the Air Line Pilots Association, is an absolutely stellar organization. They're the largest airline pilot union in the world. Every United pilot is a member. Since the 1930s, they've worked tirelessly to advocate for pilots, security, and flight safety. Their pilots flew in World War II and protected democracy. They advocated for the formation of an independent aviation safety board that led to the creation of the International Federation of Air Line

Pilots' Associations (IFALPA). They ensure that pilots are treated fairly, that flying is safe for every passenger, and that airline travel continues to grow safer. They will be guiding us through what is to come.

We spend a few hours talking with Kathi Hurst, the Event Review Committee (ERC) Chairperson at ALPA. She is an incredible woman. We walk her through everything that happened, exactly as it happened. We precisely and calmly cover everything in full detail. I'm careful to be as unemotional and factual as possible. When we finish talking, she tells us we can go ahead and contact United. She asks me if I know what I'm going to say. I do. "Lost an engine. Landed safely." That's it. Of course, they'll want me to spill my guts, but I'll tell them that I've talked to ALPA, and that we're following protocol. United knows the procedure. They'll contact ALPA's lawyers and go through the safety procedures. All they need to hear from us is that we landed safely. Kathi also tells us that we're grounded for the time being, indefinitely, until they sort out what happened. This is also protocol. She tells us that we should expect it to take the next four to six weeks, but that we'll be paid the whole time. Before she goes, she reminds us that United will ask us to take an alcohol and drug test, which is mandatory after events like these. I tell her that we had already talked about it and that we're happy to take the tests right away. We finish talking, call the station manager in, and let him know that we'd like to take our drug tests. He tells us it'll take a couple of hours to set up, but that he'll get started.

Once it's ready, we head downstairs and take the test. When we're finally done, Ed, who lives in Hawaii, heads home, and Paul and I go to a hotel—a different hotel from our original plan, because so much media had shown up at the previous hotel.

Six hours after landing, I'm finally alone. It feels strange. Such a major event had just happened. I had such a close call with such a complex and complicated situation. Hours before, I was at 36,000 feet, traveling at 550 miles per hour in the air when an engine exploded. Now I and 381 others, all still alive, are going about our day. It's as if nothing had happened. Everything is normal again.

I turn off the air-conditioning, take off my clothes, and sit on my bed in my underwear. The window is open. A nice breeze comes through. My family and I love this weather, warm with a touch of humidity. I think of them. I call my kids first, saving my girlfriend for last since I know that I'll be on that call for a while.

My kids ask me when I'm coming home. I tell them that I'm going to be hanging back until United lets us know what's next. I tell them that I'll be okay. One of my daughters is quite shaken. She followed the entire ordeal on social media. She had tried calling me when I was in the conference room, so it is nice to finally talk and let her know what's going on, that I'm okay, and that I love her. Then I spend some time talking to my girlfriend. She was so concerned and worried for me. I assure her that everything is fine and that I just need a bit of time to decompress and digest what had happened. Later, United calls to tell me that they'll be sending Paul and me back to San Francisco as passengers the next day.

I lie back on the bed, my mind still processing the events of the day. My adrenalin is still running. It feels surreal to have my feet on the ground. My head is finally on a pillow. I try to piece things together. It takes time to process something of this magnitude, but mainly, I marvel at what had happened and how three strangers could come together and deal with such an emergency. The whole crew was fantastic. They were the best pilots and flight attendants I've ever had the honor of working with. There was no ambiguity, no tension. I'm not sure what we would have done if Ed hadn't joined us that day. Questions of timing go through my mind.

What might have happened if we'd shut the engine down a few seconds later or before?

What would have happened if the cowling, when it came off, had damaged the tail?

What if?

What if?

What if?

Eventually, I drift off to sleep.

As time passes and the days continue, I don't experience any PTSD symptoms beyond these *what-ifs*. On the fourth night, I suddenly wake. I'm in a state of disbelief, yet tremendously calm. My girlfriend is now awake, and she asks me what's going on.

I had a dream, I tell her. I had dreamed that two giant hands came down from the sky and guided the airplane to the runway.

Later, people will ask me what my first thought was when this happened.

I will tell them that I prayed. "Please, God, take care of my plane, my passengers, and me."

Chapter 14

1973

Although I grew up under the Shah's regime, I still experienced a relatively open society. We had Iranian Muslims, Iranian Jews, Iranian Christians, and Iranian Bahá'ís. All different faiths were represented in Iran, and each had its own minority representative in Congress.

My dad was a nonpracticing Muslim. He never forced any of his kids into his way of thinking or belief system. We were free-spirited. He told all his children to think freely and for themselves, to do what they wanted to do, and to choose whatever they wanted to choose.

I've always been a spiritual person. My religion became the Earth and nature. I followed nature's principles from my earliest days, and I still do today. Nature does not lie. If you plant apples, you're going to get apples. If you plant carrots, you're going to get carrots. If you plant hate, you're going to get hate. If you plant love, you're going to get love. If you plant fear, you're going to get fear. If you plant success, you're going to get success. You cannot run east looking for a sunset. If that's your goal, you have to turn 180 degrees and run west.

My first real exposure to organized faith was through an American friend and neighbor in Iran. He was tall and lanky, and everyone called him Pencil. His real name was Percy. It wasn't that unusual to have an American neighbor. The United States had over 300,000 advisors in the country when I was a child. Pencil told me about the marvels of California, the weather, the girls, and the Golden Gate Bridge in San Francisco. He described the bridge like it was one of the wonders of the world—a great steel construction spanning the San Francisco Peninsula and the Marin Headlands that's brilliant reddish orange, like a deep terra cotta. Over the coming years, I'd continue my obsession with the United States and San Francisco in particular. As I learned more about the history of the city and the surrounding area, be it Alcatraz, the nearby wineries, or the ocean and mountain vistas of the Marin Headlands. Pencil was a Christian, and he'd talk to me about Christianity and faith. At the time, I didn't really have any solid path of faith. I was then, and still am, spiritual toward what I'd call the Creator or the power of the universe. But even as a child, I knew there was something out there.

Over the years, I have spent time studying the different religions of the world: Judaism, Christianity, Islam, Buddhism, and others. As I studied, I began to see ideas that were held in common belief. There is one God. There is a prophet. There are disciples. And as I continued my studies and learned that there are over 1,500 religions in the world, I realized that the Creator is not simply described in a book. The Creator has to be in your heart. It is necessary to know the universe, whoever or whatever it is you are communicating with when you are by yourself or going into meditation. When I meditate and calm my mind and center myself, I see a path, or a channel, that I can connect to the power of the universe. When I do that, I am in communion with something greater, something beyond.

Pencil taught me how to pray. I would pray for my own health, my father's, and my mother's. I was extremely worried about what I would do should one of my parents pass. My father going in and out of prison was hard on us to begin with, so I'd pray for him each night. I'd sit by my bed and pray to the Creator, and if what I prayed for became a reality, I'd say to myself, okay, this means the man upstairs is listening to me. These prayers helped me through difficult times. They taught me the importance of believing in something greater than yourself, a belief that I carried with me during the incident of Flight 1175. I carry it to this day.

Pencil also got me into motocross. Naturally, since he got me into prayer, I prayed for a bike. Eventually it worked! My mother got me one. She'd said that if I got good grades, she'd buy me one. At the time, it was about 9,000 Iranian tomans. Ironically, nowadays, one U.S. dollar is 28,000 tomans.

I doubt it was a surprise to anyone that I'd be excited by motocross. Though planes were my main focus, I was into anything mechanical. Growing up, we'd play with small remote-controlled cars. We'd race them, drive them, and take them apart and put them back together. We wanted to see how the pistons and the rings and the crankshafts worked. There was no YouTube, no Google. There were no cameras to take pictures. We'd take things apart to figure out how they worked and, as we did, we'd write everything down step-by-step so we could put it back together. Then we'd put our GI Joe soldiers in the back of little cars and drive them into trees. It was loads of fun, and we'd eventually do the same with our bikes. Taking them apart and putting them back together, that is.

The bike my mother got me that answered my prayers was a Yamaha YZ250. My friends and I all rode Yamahas. We were a scrappy bunch. We taught ourselves how to ride all throughout high school. Sometimes we'd ditch school to go riding, and if my mother asked where we'd been, I just told her we were let out of school early. I doubt she believed me.

All the bike companies had started importing their products into Iran, but, alas, there were no accessories available except for helmets. So you could buy a helmet, but not boots or shoulder pads. We had to be creative and make everything ourselves. We bought leather and took it to a seamstress or cobbler to make our jackets and pads or boots. We had our own colors. Our jackets were white with blue sleeves, and we'd put our numbers on the back. I was number 60.

We were proud of our Yamahas, so we didn't like the kids who rode Kawasakis, Suzukis, or Hondas. Each group had its own royalty. And like *West Side Story*, each neighborhood and team of bikers looked out for each other. The tension would rise every time there was a championship or race, and we had to work constantly to improve and guarantee our Yamaha victories. There were some, but I also almost lost my life.

❉ ❉ ❉

We were headed to the course to practice and play around. It was springtime. Flowers were in bloom, the air was fresh, and I was eager to get to the track. Because I practiced there so often, I decided against going through the course slowly the first time around.

What was the worst that could happen?

I knew every turn, every jump. I could visualize the entire track in my head. I knew it.

I got on my bike and rode off.

It was blissful, the wind in my face, the feeling of my Yamaha as I accelerated. The course was as I'd remembered. I took the turns and hit the jumps with confidence. But as I rounded the fifth turn and hit the jump, I went airborne. The down ramp that was supposed to be after the jump was gone! Unbeknownst to me, a small flood had come through the area, and this part of the track had been washed away.

I hit what was essentially a wall. The impact was so severe that my hands lost grip and my face smashed against the handlebar. My head was knocked back and I crumpled to the ground.

My friends saw me fall, or at least they saw me disappear and not come back. They couldn't hear my bike, so they knew something had happened, but they didn't know what. Had the bike landed on me? Crushed me? Had I broken my neck?

They rushed to me. One of my friends broke off to go bring around his green Nissan truck. Most days we'd throw our coolers and helmets and bags in the back of it, but today the truck would be for me.

I was out for a while.

When I finally came to, I saw my friends all around me. They looked concerned. They wanted to move me, but I told them not to. I tried to move my fingers, then my hands. Nothing moved.

Was this it? Would I never move again?

I just wanted to lie there and see what would happen, what I could move.

Nothing.

My friends patiently waited as 10 minutes went by. Then, very carefully, the four of them picked me up, my helmet still on, and put me in the back of the green Nissan truck. Two of them sat in the back to keep an eye on me as we drove off to the health clinic, which was four or five miles away. We passed my house on the way, and a few friends jumped off to go tell my mother what had happened. My father was in prison at the time.

In the hospital, the doctor asked me to move my fingers and hands. They shined a light in my eyes. My mother arrived, and I remember hearing the doctor tell her that I probably had a spinal cord injury and would likely never walk again. She was devastated. For the last 15 or 20 minutes before she had arrived, they had asked me to move. I couldn't. Lying in bed, I saw my dream of becoming a pilot begin to fade away. Even if I could walk again, what would happen if I couldn't pass the required physical?

I ended up staying overnight at the hospital. The next day they reexamined me. Nothing was broken, though I'd suffered a major concussion. The doctor told my mother that I just needed to rest. I was sent home in an ambulance and carried to my bedroom on a stretcher and placed in my bed. There was nothing else I could do but lie there. Over time, I started to get some feeling in my toes but not much more than that. Later, the feeling in my fingers returned. I knew then I'd make it. I was getting better, slowly but surely. I visualized myself walking. I visualized myself writing and riding and running again. I visualized myself going up to the mountains and soaring above the clouds.

While I recovered, friends would come and visit and tell me how much fun they were having riding their bikes. I knew I would be back with them soon. Bit by bit, I began to regain sensation in my body. My friends would lift me onto a stretcher and help me stand on my feet. It took time, but I built myself up until I could stand again. I never believed that my near paralysis would be a permanent thing. I always believed that I was going to overcome this situation. And once I could stand, I knew it was only a matter of time before I could walk and then run. I never let fear overtake me. That's not to say I didn't feel it. I felt fear. I knew that something was terribly wrong. I was scared when I couldn't command my hands and legs and feet and fingers to move. It's natural to feel fear, but what matters is how you respond to it. The fact that the next day I was able to wiggle my fingers and toes made me know I could get better. I would not accept being paralyzed for the rest of my life. I refused to believe that.

The injury itself was a major concussion that pushed a cervical disk in my neck just to the point of breaking—but luckily and thankfully, not past that point. If it were even just a few millimeters more, that might've been the end of it. It's these sorts of circumstances that make me feel as though I was given second chances for a reason. I survived all these close calls. I have a purpose to fulfill. Broken ribs, a broken nose, broken wrists, and broken bones were the byproducts of my motocross experiences, and these experiences formed who I am and how I persevere in the face of adversity. They never took from me my daredevil nature. I was a whirling dervish then and still am, always pushing the envelope. Once I recovered from that accident, I continued racing. My goal was, and still is, mastery at whatever I do, and I had to constantly improve if I was to become the best.

※ ※ ※

I was still riding the 250cc, but because my numbers were good, I was racing against other riders' 500cc bikes. I had the guts, but my bike just didn't have the power to compete with theirs. When the race started, they left me in the dust. There was nothing I could do about it, or so I believed. Their bikes were better than mine. As we got going, one of the bigger bikes in front of me kicked up a stone as big as a basketball into the air. It hit me in the chest and knocked me off my bike. I had broken three ribs.

After the ribs healed, I just didn't care. I'd race again. There was no question in my mind. I pushed through. The bandage was on for a week, then two weeks later I got back to racing.

Another race started. The more powerful bikes kicked up dirt. Thankfully there were no rocks to dodge. The start wasn't my best. There were about 15 other bikes in the race, and I soon found myself in 10th place. I worked my way through the pack until I was in fourth. I used my expert maneuvering ability to my advantage. Not everything was about raw power. I was only a few hundred yards behind the top three. I knew that the only way I would continue to catch up would be by technique. I had to find ways to move more efficiently and effectively around turns and over jumps. On the last leg and turn of the race, the riders in second and third places collided and fell. I passed them. Suddenly I was in second, and. I could taste first. But other bikes behind gained on me. I was hungry for a win and so were they.

I crossed the finish line. Second.

The number one guy got the win, but the cheers were for me, the underdog. Even though I didn't win, my technique and skill were apparent, even to onlookers. My team was ecstatic. They lifted me up and down. The girls went crazy. I was very popular after that. I was the comeback kid, the kind of person who comes from behind and never gives up. Often the obstacle is simply our perception of what is possible instead of what is actually possible. In times of adversity, this is essential to keep in mind. If it has been done before, you know it is possible. It might be difficult. It might not be achieved on the timeline you might imagine, but going through the obstacles is the path to success. I couldn't prevent that rock from flying up into the air, but I could control how I responded to it and recovered. You can do the same.

Chapter 15

2018

The next morning, before the flight back to San Francisco, Paul and I get breakfast. I order my favorite, two sunny-side-up eggs with ham, hash browns, and a side of sourdough toast. Paul gets the buffet.

We take our seats with our food and small-talk for a bit. We congratulate each other again and ask each other if we had spoken with our families.

We had.

We eat for a little while, both still processing the previous day.

Paul looks up from his food. He tells me he'd like to ask some questions.

"When the incident first happened, when we realized

there was an engine failure and the aircraft almost rolled over on its back, did you think that was it? We're done?"

I consider this for a second.

"Yes," I say.

Paul takes a bite to fill the silence.

If a single aspect was different, who knows what would have happened. I thought that was it. This is over. If we'd lost control at 550 miles an hour, there would have been nothing we could do.

Paul finishes his bite. "Were you okay with it? If it had happened?"

I think about my life, my family.

"Yes," I finally say. I live my life with the intention that if I put my head down at night and don't get up the next morning, I wouldn't have any regrets. I make a conscious effort to take action, to make progress. I do. I do not *try*. I don't find the word "try" useful. I never use the word "try." If someone asks you to pick up a pen that is resting on a table, you do not try to pick up the pencil, you take action and pick it up. Without action there can be no progress, and if I didn't take action the day before, we would all have died.

"What about you, Paul?" I ask. "Did you think we were going to die?"

"Absolutely. I thought, this is it," he says. "I thought we had really bought the farm. Things were out of control."

Now, I'm not certain where it originated, but in aviation, "bought the farm" refers to someone crashing and dying. Perhaps it goes back to the barnstorming days and airplanes crashing in cornfields.

"I felt the same way," he finally adds.

Once I knew I had control, once I went full deflection on the rudder and the aileron, once I pushed the nose over and brought it back, once I knew I had control of the jet, everything changed. From that point on, everything depended on me keeping the blue side up. We controlled the beast. The beast was not controlling us.

We talk for a couple more hours before it's time to get back on a plane.

We board in civilian clothes as passengers. We'd figured they'd give us first class, but, to our surprise and slight dismay, they gave us coach.

I go to the cockpit and introduce myself to the pilot. I always do this, no matter whom I'm flying with, so they know that there's a qualified airline pilot on board just in case anything should happen. I shudder to think that Ed might not have been on our flight. The pilots and cabin crew already know who we are. The flight attendants give us hugs and thank us for saving the passengers and the plane. They set us up with some better seats so we have a bit more privacy.

Paul and I talk more on the way back to San Francisco. We look over all the charts, the weather, everything. We want to make sure we have our stories straight because once we land, we'll go our separate ways. It's eerie, tracing back our journey in reverse, reliving what had just occurred with an added degree of separation. It's too much to go over on one flight, and we decide to stay in touch every couple days until things are sorted out.

Paul and I head our separate ways.

It's a relief to head home. I'm exhausted. This experience gave me, all of us on that plane, a wake-up call. We each had 40 minutes to wonder if we'd live another day, to think of all the times we should've said "I'm sorry," or "I was wrong," or "Please forgive me," or "I love you."

When I get to my house, my girlfriend is there. There are a lot of tears. She could have lost me, but there I am, and there she is. We embrace. I hold her in my arms, she holds me in hers, and I am home.

Chapter 16

1976

In 1976, I left Iran for England. My initial plan was to study there then go back to Iran and work for Iran Air. Quickly, however, that seemed unlikely.

I was 18. I had little money and didn't speak a word of English. One of my friends from the motocross days of my youth had moved to London, and I was blessed to be able to spend a week with him as I got acclimated.

It was all so strange to me, a massive city full of strangers. The weather where I'd come from was wonderful. It was sunny, like the high mountains in Colorado. London was foggy and cold and gray. I'd never seen fog before. It was mesmerizing to walk through, watching the yellow glow of London streetlamps wavering through the fog. In Iran, the lights all seemed to be incredibly bright and fluorescent, but the lights of England had a dim and yellow quality to them. I enjoyed those walks. I could get used to them. Unfortunately, at the end of my first week, my friend told me that he couldn't take care of me. I decided to go southwest of London to Bournemouth. There I would learn English.

My friend drove me down there and I talked to a school about signing up for classes. I told them who I was and where I came from. I registered for classes. I had no place to stay, but I didn't have time to worry. Worrying wouldn't solve anything.

I didn't have much money, and the school suggested I check the bulletin board for housing opportunities. I found a studio for 10£ a week that was a 10-minute walk from class. It was just one room with a little stove and toaster oven. I had to share a toilet with the other people in the building. But it was home.

\#

It was a time of turmoil for Iran. During my earlier teens, my father was still gone a great deal, imprisoned due to his beliefs and his political allies. It goes without saying that my father's years of political activities were very difficult for my mother. She didn't know his whereabouts when he was arrested. She was constantly going from office to office, prison to prison, asking where her husband was. They never gave correct answers. When she went to

Evin Prison, they said he was in the police department's prison. When she went to the police department's prison, they said that he was in Gasr Prison. They constantly gave her the runaround.

My father was a professor and earned a good salary, but under Iranian law, if a person is imprisoned, especially a political prisoner, their salary is withheld from their family. While my father was gone, my mother had to keep us all fed and take care of our needs. Her perseverance was inspiring. She had no help with us while my father was away, and she never asked for any. She would sell her jewelry to try and make ends meet, but selling household items didn't always cover the expenses. My mom was a housewife and mother, formidable jobs, especially with a husband often languishing in prison. I've never known a more compassionate and loving person. She embraced life, her husband, and her children with such undiminishing vigor and an open heart that it became an impenetrable barrier between us and the darkness of the times. She never made us feel unloved nor blamed my father for the predicament we found ourselves in. She was a rock for us all.

Once, when I was 8 years old, she took me to the university where my father used to work to talk to the president of the university and get my father's unpaid salaries. Mrs.

Parsa, the president of the university, was a dignified and kind woman, but said there was nothing she could do.

Tears welled up in my mother's eyes.

What happened next changed my worldview.

Mrs. Parsa took her checkbook out of her bag and wrote my mother a personal check. I couldn't believe it. I'd never witnessed this kind of generosity from a stranger. Seeing that a stranger could be so kind and thoughtful was such a gift for me. It was the first time in my life I experienced help from a total stranger. Later, she'd become the minister of education, but tragically, after the revolution, she was brutally beaten and then executed for having worked in the Shah's government. She was an incredible woman. Her kindness changed our lives. As she wrote the check, she looked at me and said, "Son, don't worry. Everything is going to be okay. You're going to do many great things."

And she was right.

Of course, my response at the time was more along the lines of "What do you know?" I was only eight years old. But she was right. More importantly, her actions taught me that someone other than my family cared about what happened to my father and to us. It made an impression on me that I will never forget.

Unfortunately, while our struggle was profound, it was not a unique situation. Many families and people suffered similar fates. Families were in crisis, broken apart by ideologies. On top of that, due to my father's frequent incarcerations, my mother feared that I might be targeted. My dream to fly for Iran Air seemed impossible at the time. So the decision was made to send me out of the country to go to school in the USA. I wasn't able to get a student visa to go to the States, but I was able to get one to go to England. We didn't know anything. Nobody had done any research. There was no time. I just needed to get out. My dad knew that the revolution was going to happen, something was going to turn against the Shah. It was only a matter of time.

Three years after I left, in 1979, there would be a revolution. The government would be toppled, and the ayatollahs would take over. I would be told not to come back, that things were still changing. Soon after, Saddam Hussein of Iraq attacked Iran, and my fate was sealed. I would not be going back. If I did, I would likely have been drafted into the army and killed. It was a tragic war with almost a million young killed on both sides.

❅ ❅ ❅

After finishing my English classes, I headed off to Newbury College where I finished my degree in physics. I absolutely love science. It goes back to my fascination as a kid with anything mechanical. Mathematics, physics, and engineering are, in part, what makes flight, and so much more, possible. However, once in England, it quickly became apparent that my dream of becoming a pilot was no more possible in England than in Iran. During those days there were only three airlines: British Overseas Airway Commissions (BOAC), British Airways, and British Caledonian (which was taken over by British Airways in 1988). British Airways was the biggest, and at the time they had no foreign pilots. However, I did have a chance to speak with a British Airways pilot. He lived in the town Thatcham, which was a town over from me. He flew a 737. The first thing I noticed when I met with him was that he drove a beautiful Lancia Montecarlo sports car. We got in and drove off into the British countryside going nice and fast. We ended up at a pub. He bought me a beer and listened to my story and my passion for becoming a pilot.

When I finished my story, he told me that there were hardly any jobs available in England. There simply weren't that many airlines. He told me that I needed to go to the United States, because in the U.S. there were over a hundred airlines and that I should have little trouble getting a job as a pilot there. It was clear that I'd need to go to

Chapter 16

America to achieve my dream, but for the time being, I was in England.

England in 1976 was not the country it is now. There were not many foreigners, especially in the small town of Newbury. I stuck out like a sore thumb. However, I was lucky enough to have found some Iranian friends: Edwin and Reza. The three of us quickly grew close. We'd hang out together, play badminton, go swimming. Well, I'd go swimming; they mainly went to see girls in their bikinis. Reza ended up being the first among us to find a girlfriend and, as is common, he began spending more and more time with her. I didn't have much time for that. Then as now, I was very athletic. I'd sneak in runs during lunchtime. I kept pushing myself in sports and school to keep my mind off what was going on back home. I even ran with a group of teachers and became friends with many of them. It was part of my deep drive to connect with people who knew more than I did. After our runs, we'd hang around and grab a sandwich or a water and we'd talk. I wasn't just hanging around with average school kids. I wasn't going to fall into partying and drinking and doing drugs. I would have a drink every now and again but still, to this day, I've never been drunk. I was then, and still am, always pursuing excellence.

A physics teacher of ours, Mrs. Pierce, was sympathetic to what we were going through. She was a gentle soul.

While some students called us names and told us to go back to our country or to go ride camels, she always stood up for us. Our country was going through an uprising. There was so much death in our lives and there we were in England, away from our families. She let us know that she understood what was going on. She told us that the average English person didn't understand what we were going through, that they didn't have to work hard for anything, at least not the way we had to. They didn't understand what it felt like to be separated from one's family in the way that we were. They could go home and visit their parents any time they wanted. She made us feel seen, and it was a wonderful feeling. When I told her that I had decided to go to the United States to become a pilot, she was delighted. We stayed in touch over the years, writing letters to each other. She was a wonderful woman and a dear friend and teacher, but unfortunately, twenty years ago, she passed. I will never forget the impact she had on me.

❈ ❈ ❈

University was a rough yet formative time. It's time I mention my martial arts training, which I began in Iran when I was in my preteens. I had just seen my first Bruce Lee movie and I was utterly taken by him—how one person could fight so many people. I always thought that martial arts would be fun, plus it would be a deterrent to people who wanted to mess with me. So I began my training. My parents couldn't help much. It's not that they were against it; they just had other things to worry about. My dad wasn't around most of the time and my mother was busy taking care of the family. It wasn't like in America, where parents take the kids from volleyball to basketball to soccer to martial arts. Iranian parents didn't chauffeur kids around. I had to do it myself. I wanted to spend as much time at the dojo (the martial arts school) as I could and learn from those more advanced than me. No one else in my neighborhood did martial arts at the time, so I couldn't ask for a ride. I had to take the bus there and back.

I eventually discovered a kid in a nearby neighborhood was also training in martial arts, and we started taking the bus together. Outside of class, I'd work and practice my katas, or forms. I loved how in Shotokan, the art I studied, when doing katas, you end where you begin. You come full circle. So much of life is like that. I loved all of it—the uniforms, the structure, the order, the testosterone, the young guys screaming. I'd have my cousin, the same one who fell through the roof and into the outhouse ditch in the countryside, hold a really thick pillow and I'd practice my kicks. He'd fly across the room. It was great fun. I kept training and learning and practicing, and by the time I left Iran I was a green belt.

Back to England. I'd found a nearby martial arts club that trained in Shotokan. Classes were held in a high school gym after school hours. We had it to ourselves. There were about 25 students who'd line up by seniority of rank from left to right: white, yellow, green, purple, brown, and then black. Since I was already a green belt, I lined up in middle. I was fast and tall, thin and athletic. I weighed maybe 180 pounds at six-foot-two. I had an extra-long reach and would supersize everything I did. I'd always go the extra mile. When I thew punches, I put my entire body behind it so the momentum would take me about another foot forward. Other students weren't used to sparring this way. They'd stand four feet away thinking I wouldn't reach them, but I would. I moved up quickly in the ranks. I earned my purple belt, and then brown. Since I loved it so much, I began teaching, and before leaving England, I finally got my black belt.

The head instructor, Sensei David Jones, became a good friend of mine. Martial arts gave me a community in England that I could be a part of. In Iran, I was the only person in my high school who practiced martial arts. People would tease me about it, but I never used my martial arts against anyone; never got into a fight because of it. In Shotokan, everyone is accepted. Your background doesn't matter. We all trained toward mastery. David continued training long after our time in university, and he still practices today. He became an eighth-degree black belt and is the chief instructor at the Calgary International Shotokan Karate Federation (ISKF) and the chairman of ISKF Canada. We've stayed good friends. He made martial arts his way of life as I would go on to make aviation mine. But martial arts never fully left my life. I eventually achieved my third-degree black belt.

※ ※ ※

The animosity that Edwin, Reza, and I felt in England wasn't just at school. In the mid-'70s, England wasn't as cosmopolitan or foreigner-friendly as it is now. I stood out, especially in a small town like Newbury. A lot of Arabs would come through as well as Pakistanis and Indians. People really had hatred toward them and us. We were put in the same category.

For me, it was a bit of a double-edged sword. I did martial arts, and nobody really tried to say anything bad to me. I don't think it was because I was tough, but rather because the students had learned to respect someone who conveyed authority. When I wasn't in class or playing sports or in a competitive environment—when I was just walking the streets—people looked at me as if something were wrong with me. It was awful. These shared hardships brought Edwin, Reza, and me even closer together. The three of us were all only sons in our families, and we were all here in England on our own trying to make something happen. We hadn't known each other before. We'd all lived and created our own lives, but we became our own best friends. I had my martial arts friends and my running team, but the rest of the time the three of us hung out together. We were each other's support systems.

One day in the middle of my time at university—I was 19—Reza got in a car with his girlfriend. They drove down a dual carriageway, which is two roads separated by a median strip. Something happened and Reza hit the brakes.

Their car skidded off and went into the other lane.

It was a head-on collision.

They both died instantly.

It was tragic and shook me to the core. Edwin was closer to Reza than I was. They both smoked, so they spent a bit more time together. They'd spend afternoons on the campus lawn, talking and laughing and smoking and checking out girls while I went for runs. But I couldn't run from this. Reza's death was such a terrible loss. A key part of my support system had disappeared, vanished, died. I couldn't believe I was saying goodbye to a friend I had just seen the night before.

Chapter 16

He was staying with a British family. They were the ones who contacted me and told me what had happened. They asked me to break the news to his family. It was early afternoon, and we were outside on the street. I got off the phone and told Edwin what had happened.

He started screaming and yelling. He couldn't believe it. He was grieving so loudly. Everyone noticed. He was grieving from the top of his lungs. Loss touches such depths within oneself. We Persians do not keep it quiet. We are very emotional people. I had to be a support system for Edwin.

Later I was contacted by the brother of Reza's girlfriend. I had to go identify the body. Edwin couldn't bring himself to do it, so I went alone.

There were a lot of internal injuries, but the face was not deformed. Reza looked like a typical Iranian kid at the time. His hair was a little long, maybe down to the bottom of his neck. He had a mustache and a nice clean beard. It was really well shaped. We all took really good care of our hair. They used to call us pretty boys because we always dressed well and smelled good and were well groomed. Reza looked so peaceful. He was very, very pale, but so incredibly peaceful. It was eerie.

He was dead.

The shock fully hit me then.

I looked at him. I told them, yes, this is my friend. I told them who he was. They asked if we were related.

I told them, no, that we were just friends.

As I was leaving, I kissed him on the forehead and held his hand. I squeezed it and told him I was sorry, that I was so incredibly sorry. He had such goodness about him. He was barely 19 years old. I kept saying sorry, again and again and again.

When I signed the paper confirming his identity, they told me that I'd need to contact Reza's family. I told them that his family was in Iran and that he had nobody here. But doing nothing wasn't an option. I needed to do something. I had to contact them. They needed to know, and they needed to be able to make the arrangements for his funeral. I wasn't fully sure what to do, but I told them I'd figure it out and I did just that.

I had the telephone number of his home back in Iran. I called. Reza's mother answered. Before I even heard her voice, my heart broke for her. But I had to be strong. The operator spoke first. "Ma'am, this is the operator. There is a call for you from overseas." I imagine there was some degree of suspense on her end. Maybe she thought her son was calling.

I politely introduced myself and told her that I needed to talk to her husband.

Chapter 16

She told me he was working.

I asked when he was coming home. I didn't want to break the news to her. In those days, it was customary to talk to the man of the house so he could decide how he to tell the rest of the family.

She told me when he'd be home.

I asked if it would be okay for me to call back then.

She asked if everything was okay.

I told her that it was, that everything was fine, and I just needed to talk with her husband.

We talked a little bit more. She asked how I'd been, and what I was up to. She'd spoken with her son the week before. I had to lie. I couldn't bring myself to tell her. I wanted to show respect as I had been taught, that we should always talk to the man of the house.

I said goodbye and hung up.

The wait felt incredibly long.

It was torturous.

I was to call back around three in the afternoon the next day. The wait was horrible.

Outside the college was a park that the three of us would go to. It was a beautiful wooded area with plenty of fresh air and chirping birds. There was this trail in the park, and we'd sit by a broken tree and pick at the bark and chat. The guys would smoke. We'd bullshit and laugh. I miss those times.

I drove to Edwin's house to pick him up. We grabbed sandwiches and went to the park. The walk to the tree was so lonely. We sat by our tree. It felt wrong. Reza wasn't there. Our friend wasn't there. Instead of three, there were only two. Edwin was still very emotional. He was smoking and swearing, cursing at everything. Even though I tried to hold it back, I teared up. To this day, I still tear up thinking about my friend. I knew that the next call was going to be so incredibly difficult. I was going to have to tell my good friend's parents that their only son was dead. We were all only sons. We all had hopes and dreams to do certain things for our families. We all wanted to achieve great things and become productive members of society. We wanted to make our parents proud. We spent a few hours talking and reflecting on things by that tree.

Then it was time. I headed back to my apartment and found a pay phone. I couldn't wait or put it off any longer. The public phones operated with coins, and I had plenty, 2£ or 3£, just in case the call went long. I didn't want to have to tell them I'd run out of time. It was only the day after the accident. The least I could do was buy them all the time that I could.

Chapter 16

I placed the call.

Reza's mother picked up and I asked to speak with her husband.

I said hello.

He asked how Reza and I were.

There it was. The moment I'd been dreading. I told him there was something I needed to tell him.

He asked if Reza wasn't doing well in school.

I told him no, that I had tell him that something really bad had happened, that there had been an accident. I wasn't sure how to say it. My heart was racing. Finally the silence broke. He asked me how bad the accident was. I said that they had a head-on collision and that his son had died immediately.

I paused.

His father asked if he was okay.

It was hard to find the words. I took a deep breath and told him that they both died instantly.

He paused.

I could hear that he had begun to cry. I could hear Reza's mother in the background sobbing. She must've been next to him or was able to hear what I'd told her husband.

It was heartbreaking. I still tear up thinking about it.

It went on like this for a couple of minutes. No words were spoken. Only tears.

I was crying too. We were all at such a loss of words.

Once he was able to speak again, Reza's father asked me if I saw the body. I told him that I didn't see the body after the accident, but that I had seen his son the next morning. I shared the story of going to the morgue and identifying the body.

We spoke again the next day. Reza's father told me that they wanted to bring the body home. They wanted me to help get Reza back to his family. They told me they'd pay for everything and that I just needed to make the arrangements since I was in England. I told them I would do that. I contacted the hospital. There needed to be a coffin and they had to wrap him properly and I had to make arrangements with the airlines. It was British Airways. I went to the airport to see him off. No pictures were taken to send to the family. I made sure that I got all the proper paperwork. I was given power of attorney to sign for everything. There was no seat number; just a cargo bill. In holding that bill, I held my friend. Watching Reza's coffin being pulled away, I thought about what was going to happen to his family. What might happen once the plane landed in Iran. It hurt that I wouldn't know.

To this day, I have not been back to Iran. I've flown a lot

of bodies, especially during the war with Iraq in 2003. I've flown a lot of caskets to different parts of the world. These were mainly domestic flights on the way to some Navy or Air Force town. I'm particularly emotional when I know a soldier is there with us. When I land, I can see the grieving people. They're waiting there when I get off the airplane. Everyone's head is down. It's very somber. I feel so much for families that have lost their child, or children, to war. I don't believe that anyone has the right to take another person's life except God. It's not for us for humans to do. Accidents happen, but I don't believe in wars. I don't believe in dying for some ridiculous cause or for some political game. I believe that we are able to create a better world. It just takes one person with one thought, a thought that spreads and can be built upon. I believe change is possible.

Reza was such a dear friend. He was like me. He understood where I came from in ways others could not, and I lost him. This was the first time someone close to me had died. I couldn't imagine the pain and agony that his family must be going through. As a 19-year-old, I wasn't sure how to deal with it either. I realized that life can be taken away from you at any moment, but that life continues. You get up and you go to school. You exercise and you work and time passes. Decades later, when my father passed, everything just continued. I take this all to mean that you should live your life as best as you can, to live and play as hard as you can, because once you're gone, you're gone. There is no guarantee.

※ ※ ※

School was coming to a close. The prospect of getting to the United States loomed before me. I did some research and found a flight school in Oakland, California. My sights were set on the San Francisco Bay Area. My martial arts instructor Dave and I had become quite close by this time, and he had decided to join me.

When I told Edwin I was leaving, he said he wanted to leave as well. Unfortunately, he couldn't. Not many people could at the time. Edwin ended up going to Toronto, Canada. We stayed in touch for a little while, but eventually we lost touch.

Dave got his tourist visa quite easily. Mine was a bit more of a problem.

The first time I drove out from my little town to London to go to the American embassy to apply for a visa, I was denied. The American Embassy in Tehran had been overrun by militant students who took embassy employees hostage. So being Iranian and applying to get into the United States was difficult. I waited six months, as was required, and applied again.

I was denied.

I brought paperwork showing that I had the $40,000 in my account, but they implied it wasn't enough. I left. But I came back, still showing that paper—even though the money was gone. I was denied three times, but I never gave up. The fourth time, the lady recognized me. She'd seen that I had kept coming, and she correctly assumed that I would do so again and again. I told her, "This is my destiny. I must go and become an airline pilot."

She looked me in the eyes and told me, "You know what? I appreciate your dreams. Your tenaciousness, your intensity." She asked me to make one promise—that when I got to the United States I wouldn't depend on the government.

"When I go?" I asked.

"Yes," she said. "Go. Make something of yourself. Go after your dream and live it."

I made that promise and I kept it.

Chapter 17

2018

There aren't many jobs where you go to work and might never return. Arriving home, something realigns inside me. I just want to hold my girlfriend in my arms. I struggle to fall asleep that night. I tell my girlfriend of my urge to leave everything behind and get a backpack and head off Kilimanjaro or Everest or Denali. I want to escape.

❊ ❊ ❊

Another incident came to mind after Flight 1175. When living in Florida, I purchased a sailboat. I've been sailing for more than 35 years. Even though I frequently take my kids out, I also enjoy solo sailing. I have a deep fascination for the ocean and great respect for its power and might. Even when moored, the gentle rocking of a boat brings me peace. But anyone who's ever gone out on the ocean knows that those tranquil moments can change in an instant. I learned how to sail, the way I learn most things, full-out.

The Gulf Stream off South Florida flows south to north, and the wind flows against it, causing the seas to be fairly rough. On this day, the forecast was for four- to five-foot waves, which isn't too big of a deal. It was an idyllic day. I was alone with my thoughts and the beautiful water. As I left the shore behind, I watched the gulls fly above. They performed a beautiful ballet, soaring on the thermals as they searched for food.

I sailed on. The boat performed beautifully, and I knew all was well.

But soon clouds started to bank up. Dark clouds. The northerly winds changed and became stronger. Sure enough, a storm moved in, and I was headed straight for it. Far from shore at this point, I knew I needed to come about and head for land. The storm grew in intensity and waves grew to 15 feet. They swelled and crashed over the deck. I was alone with my boat, my thoughts, and the storm. I realized I was about to be tested again. The jaws of the storm bore down on me. The strength and power of the ocean are immeasurable. When sailing, man pits himself against the forces of nature, and on that dark afternoon, I had a formidable battle to wage. I sailed on. I made it to shore.

✽ ✽ ✽

I wake up in the middle of the night. Questions race through my mind.

What if the wing had fallen off?

What if part of the engine that had separated at 550 miles per hour had hit the tail? If the tail had been knocked off, the plane would have rolled over and we would have all been dead.

I think about how the engines are tested, and how blocks of ice and frozen birds are thrown in to see if they can withstand the damage.

I think about what might have happened if pieces of the cowling had come off and struck the plane.

My mind goes to the cockpit and how chaotic everything was.

What if there were major checklists we had missed?

What if I had found myself alone flying that plane?

What if Paul or Ed hadn't been there?

My thoughts are chaotic, but eventually, I make sense of them. I make it through the storm. I come up with something that I call "the five stars." These are the five stars that lined up that day for us to safely land.

Star 1: Three minutes before the incident and the engine blowing up, I was outside the cockpit using the bathroom. If we'd lost even seconds, the plane could easily have become an uncontrollable missile that we would never have been able to get back. The airplane rolled and we acted in one and a half seconds.

Star 2: Ed Gagarin rode in the jump seat in the cockpit. Ed is a United pilot and had finished his IOE (Initial Operating Experience) on the Boeing 777. Having just finished training, he was sharp and on top of his game. Ed was truly instrumental to the success of that flight.

Star 3: We were only 40 minutes and 200 miles out from Honolulu. After the investigators fed the information from the FDR (Flight Data Recorder) into the computer and the simulator, we were told that if we had been an hour out—300—miles—this would have been a controlled descent into the water with full thrust on the left engine.

Star 4: More than a thousand pounds of metal and material came off that engine, and not a single fragment hit the tail. At 550 miles an hour, even 10 pounds hitting the tail could have ripped the tail off.

Star 5: A blade actually came off the engine and hit the fuselage. Fortunately, it hit the strongest point, which is called the stringers. You can compare it to a rib cage on the human body. It made a dent, but it did not penetrate the skin. A few inches up, and it would have gone through a window. A few inches forward, and it would have gone through the skin of the airplane. In either case, it would have depressurized the aircraft, and our checklist would have called for a rapid descent to 10,000 feet. At 120 miles out, we would not have made Honolulu Airport.

Without these five stars, these answered prayers, we might not have been able to return to our families. I have the dream where the great hands of the Creator guide us down from the sky to safety. It wasn't my hands on the yoke and throttle, it was a force and presence greater than me or any human. I think about what it would have been like if we didn't make it. The things that would have been left unsaid, left undone. My thoughts of seeing my family again saw me through those harrowing minutes up in the air. I can only imagine how others felt, not having any control over what was happening.

During the coming days, I'm more internal, and less talkative. I wander around the garden. It's February and cold. I want to be alone. I sit. I meditate.

❇ ❇ ❇

Meditation has been a part of my life since I started martial arts in Iran at 11. Before class, the sensei, or teacher, would call out "mokuso," pronounced "mok'so," meaning silent meditation. We'd take several moments and use breathing techniques to clear our minds before training. We'd do the same at the end of class to relax and decompress and center ourselves. I would continue this practice on and off throughout my life, just as I continued martial arts training, but it was about 20 years ago when I got more involved in meditation. I was taking a yoga class and after one of the sessions, I approached the instructor and told her that I'd been studying martial arts for 30 years and teaching it, but that I wasn't particularly familiar with meditation. She also didn't know much about it. When she told the class to meditate, she expected each student to do their own thing. So I started doing research. I read books and listened to audiotapes and began to learn more and more about meditation.

One of the meditation techniques that spoke to me was called the golden elevator. It's one that I've since adapted to my own needs and still practice to this day. I begin by imagining that I'm in a hotel lobby. I'm on the second floor, and I look down to the ground level and I see this golden elevator. I head over to the elevator, and I get inside. I press the button for the lowest level and go down and down and down and down into the deepest, darkest space in the Earth, like Moria in *Lord of the Rings*, where Gandalf fell to the Balrog. I go further still, down deeper and deeper into the darkness. I lose track of time. Then finally, the golden elevator stops. The door opens into a room. I step out of the golden elevator. There is a door in front of me with my name on it. I approach the door, open it, and go inside. The lights go on and my eyes adjust. I see posters on the walls of all the things I want in life. I see them. I visualize them. I head through a passageway and catch fire. It fills me entirely and kills off all the bad stuff in my mind. I continue through the fire and out into the snow. I lie down and wait for the fire to go out. My entire body becomes a snowman and I walk to a lake. There I immerse myself in the water. The snow begins to melt until I'm one with the water. I am surrounded by it. I swim through the lake, and on the other side emerge as a blue human full of water. I'm walking again. I walk through a waterfall, and I emerge, as a human once again, onto a road. At the end of the road is a modest, two-story white house. An old gentleman is waiting for me. He puts a cape around my back and hands me a walking stick. He puts a crown on my head and adorns me in gold and guides me to the house. He leads me to the second floor where millions of people are standing, looking for guidance, and with them, I begin to share.

I open my eyes.

I do this at night before bed, and you can do it too. I lie down and put on music. It can be any music that you find calming and relaxing. I start breathing and I begin the golden elevator. We have so much going on around us, so much chaos, so much stimulation. It's important to find the space in our day where spirituality can come in and you can experience the power of the Creator. It's akin to the state you feel when you go marvel at the cedars in the mountains, at the reflections of the sky in the lake, at the vibrant colors of a perfect sunset, or the warmth of the sun as you cross the Golden Gate Bridge. It just brings you down to earth. Man gets tired of what man makes, or it grows old, but you never tire of a perfect sunset or sunrise.

❈ ❈ ❈

My thoughts also go to my father. He's struggling with cancer. I tell my sisters not to tell him anything about my harrowing flight yet. I want to talk him through what happened in person. I don't want him to worry between the time he learns of what happened and when he can speak with me.

The next morning, I wake up. My girlfriend, Maleah, does too. I have the weirdest feeling. I was dreaming about what had happened up there. My mind, again, goes to the two giant hands coming out of the clouds, holding the air under the wings and engines and guiding us toward the airport. I feel pulled toward the spiritual. I still want to flee with a backpack to the mountains. I decide to take a few days and visit my children.

I drive to Southern California to visit my oldest daughter

and son. My daughter is thrilled to see me. As soon as I park and get out of the car, she runs to me. We hold each other for almost 15 minutes without saying a word. We both cry, both fully embracing human connection. We go and get dinner, then Maleah and I stay at the *Queen Mary* boat in Long Beach. It's a nice evening, but very cold. Santa Ana winds are blowing. We spend the first half of the next day there before driving up the coast to visit my son. We take him out to dinner. It's lovely to spend time with them all.

I see my father. I tell him the whole story.

He tells me that he's very happy and pleased that I was behind the controls of the jet. He tells me he believes in me, in my strength, that his blood runs through my veins. These words mean the world to me. He has always been an incredibly strong man. He has always stood tall, with firm resolve. He knew that I wouldn't give up. He tells me not to worry about a thing and that everything will be okay. "You'll do great things in life," he says.

A few months later he will pass on.

❆ ❆ ❆

My father passes on May 6, 2018. It's a couple of months after my accident with United. I'm flying back from Honolulu to Denver. There's something strange in the air. Every spring when I fly from Honolulu to Denver, eastbound, I always see Venus come up on the horizon. This night it's particularly bright. The skyline is gorgeous. The setting sun paints the sky hundreds of different colors, from purple to yellow and blue to red. But as Venus comes higher above the horizon, maybe 10 or 15 degrees, it becomes like this very bright star.

I land and take out my phone. I have a text from my sister. She wants me to contact her immediately. Our father is in the hospital. They don't think he's going to make it.

I call United right away, and they take me off my flight and try to put me on the next one back home. Unfortunately, there's no next flight, so I go on Southwest Airlines in the jump seat to Sacramento. I'm very emotional.

I arrive in Sacramento. Maleah picks me up and we go directly to the hospital. I tell her to drop me off. I'll figure out how to get home.

My father passes away five minutes before I get there. Such unbelievable sorrow and sadness and anger overtake me. My father is gone. I wish, so deeply, that I'd been there the last few minutes. I'd had a feeling on this trip that something was going to happen. I'd told everybody to let me know immediately if he started to get worse, if it seemed like something would happen. I wanted to be there for the last few hours with him. But it didn't happen.

I see my father, lying there with his eyes closed. I kiss him. I cry a lot. My sisters are there too. We talk of our life with our father and of all the terrible things he had gone through and what beautiful principles he stood for. We talk to him and stay with him for about a half hour. They want to transfer him to a movable bed. They ask if we'd like to help. My two sisters and I pick him up. His back is still warm. It's a strange sensation. We lift him off his bed and put him on the movable one. They wheel him away. I stay in the hallway until I can no longer see him. It's one of the toughest moments of my life. It's so painful to have this man taken from us. He brought me into this world. He was my rock, and he was such an amazing and decent and kind human being who had never harmed anyone. All he wanted to do was help everyone around him. He wanted to help his country.

I long for him to still be here, to guide me, to motivate me. I think about him every day. Growing up in a troubled Iran left a mark on my heart. All that my father went through, the prisons, the tortures, the deprivations of being away from his family for years, the hunger, the lack of justice, lead me to reevaluate things. He was a stubborn man who stood up for his beliefs. He was a mighty man to me. He was my father, and his death leaves a hole in my heart that will never be filled.

Chapter 18

1979

I'd found a flight school in the San Francisco Bay Area that was accepting students. My dream was getting closer to reality. I didn't pause to think about the obstacles that might get in my way. I didn't program my mind with negativity. I stayed laser-focused on the prize of a commercial pilot's license. I didn't worry about rent, a job, or paying tuition.

Too often we get bogged down in the details of how we are to accomplish goals when things appear bleak or impossible. Giving up is easier when we succumb to negativity. I've learned that we must focus on one step, one day at a time, never veering from the true north of our destiny and dreams.

That is what I did.

I visualized myself landing in San Francisco and going

through school and getting my pilot's license. I could see it, and I knew it would happen. If you cannot see it, if you cannot see yourself achieving your dreams, you will not succeed.

❊ ❊ ❊

We ended up flying into San Francisco on a Pan Am 747. I made sure of it. I wouldn't let us fly to the United States any other way. It was the airplane that set my heart on aviation, and it would be the plane to take me to the next destination of my journey. On the flight, I listened to some music. Surfing through the programming on the armrest, I settled on Kenny Rogers and listened to an entire album on the way to San Francisco. I was giddy and my heart was set. I knew it was only a matter of time before I'd be piloting a 747 myself.

When we landed at the San Francisco International Airport, Kenny Rogers was still playing in our heads. Outside the terminal, suitcases in hand, we paused and asked ourselves: Now what? Suddenly, it all felt real.

We flagged down a taxi and got inside. The driver was Indian. He asked us where we'd like to go. Dave and I had to pause again. We didn't know where we were going. We told the driver that we were new to the country, that we didn't know anyone, but we needed to find a place to stay, a hotel probably. He told us that he had a cousin

Chapter 18

who owned a place just off Bush and Van Ness. It was in a large Victorian home called Shangri La.

On the ride to Shangri La, I felt for my wallet. I had only $200. At the time, Iran was in the middle of a revolution. The country was at war and my money was cut off. Other than the money in my pocket, all I had was a letter from a bank that my dad got for me. It declared that I'd be able to cover the costs of my private pilot's license. It didn't even cover the training; just the license. I still needed to come up with $40,000 to cover the tuition. But that was a concern for another time. I'd have to work hard, no question about it, but this type of struggle never bothered me. I knew the value of hard work and that there were kind people in this world.

We soon arrived at Shangri La. We managed to get a room for the whole month for around $100, which Dave paid for. I was so excited and high on my dream. We'd found our base. We'd arrived, and San Francisco awaited.

I had told myself that I was going to enjoy my first month in California because once I started flying school, I knew I wouldn't have the money or time to do anything else. When I went to the Sierra Academy of Aeronautics and registered, they asked when I'd be starting. I told them that I'd be back in three weeks. Meanwhile, Dave started applying for jobs, but without a green card, he was having trouble, and his visa was only good for a few months. He had no plan nor desire to return to England, so he did some research and found out that, as a British citizen, he could go to Canada without a green card or a work permit and still qualify for residency. So that was that. We'd have the month together before my flight school and his move to Canada.

California was dazzling to me. I remember the first time we went across the Golden Gate Bridge. We were in awe. Even before I'd moved to the U.S., I was high on America and the American dream and California in particular. I'd marveled at pictures of San Francisco and the Golden Gate Bridge, of Alcatraz Island, and the flowered twists and turns of Lombard Street. But now it was all real. I could see it, smell it. I felt the opportunities in the sunshine. There is a Persian expression that basically says if you visualize something you want to have or a place you want to visit, it's almost half the fun of being there. And then when you go, and you experience it, it's even better. And was it ever.

Dave wanted to go to Universal Studios. He'd purchased a yellow Pontiac like in *Starsky and Hutch* and we drove down to Los Angeles. Within the first hundred miles of our road trip, we were pulled over by a cop. We weren't sure what to do. Were they going to arrest us? Something worse?

The officer came over and spoke with us. Now, Dave had grown up in London and was used to driving on the left side of the road. He had been swerving in his struggle to stay in the right lane, and the cop had thought we were drunk. We apologized and explained to him that we'd just come from England. He told us to be careful and not to kill anyone. We were lucky to be left off with a warning.

We made it to Los Angeles and to Universal Studios. Afterward, we went on a tour that took us to the homes of movie stars. It was thrilling to be in the same city where these larger-than-life stars I'd followed my whole life lived. Suddenly they were just people. It can be easy to forget that sometimes. Seeing them in films, it's hard not to put them up on a pedestal. I told Dave I was going to come back to Hollywood one day and make my own movie.

One night, closer to when Dave had to leave, we went to a nightclub in San Francisco. There were a couple of really good-looking girls, and so, of course, we started talking to them. I told them that I'd come to the United States to go to a flight academy in Oakland. As luck would have it, one of them told me that she had a cousin who lived 10 minutes from the Oakland airport and that we should meet. She put me in touch, and he became my first new—and soon to be one of my best—friends. His name was Ron Tom, and he had a two-bedroom apartment in San Leandro with a spare room. It was perfect, especially because our month was about to be up at Shangri La, and I only had to pay about $50 a month. Ron soon became one of my biggest cheerleaders. Ron never finished school. He'd struggled through high school, and he worked stocking shelves in a small grocery store his father owned. But he kept pushing me and telling me to go after aviation, to go after schooling. "That's your ticket up," he'd tell me. "I'll support you any way I can." And so he did. I always say that all you need in life is a friend or someone who believes in you. With that, and if you believe in yourself, you can do anything in life. You are never defeated until you accept defeat.

Chapter 19

2018

I get a phone call from Kathi Hurst and ALPA. She lets me know that there's going to be a conference call with representatives from United, ALPA, the FAA, and the NTSB (National Transportation Safety Board). There will be 33 questions. They've listened to the Black box CVR (Cockpit Voice Recording), and they want to hear from us that our story matches. The investigation is coming to a close, and soon we'll know what really happened to the plane. After a couple of weeks, we get another call from Kathi.

Before the call, my mind goes through moments of crisis in my life. These are thoughts not of anxiety, but of reflection and gratitude. My mind flashes back to the incident en route to Honolulu, and how my instincts kicked in. *Aviate. Fly the airplane. Navigate. Go to the point where I want to go. Communicate. Make sure air traffic control knows what's going on.* People can get this wrong. People have gotten this wrong. It doesn't matter how well you communicate if you fail to navigate and fly the plane into the side of a mountain. The order of these ideas is important. The first thing they teach you when you start to fly is to keep the blue side up and not to hit anything. Even if you lose your engine, you can still glide the airplane. If you can't go to your intended destination, you can find a different one, a clear stretch of road or another airport. Once that's in process, you proceed to the next step: communicating what's going on with air traffic control. These basic principles are where my mind went when the engine blew up. The plane rolled and banked at a 45-degree angle, and the first thing was to keep the blue side up, roll out of the bank, and fly the airplane straight and level. Next up was navigate. We were supposed to go to a waypoint and then turn right to Honolulu, but that didn't happen. Instead of going left for 20 or 30 miles and then turning right, I decided to go straight to Honolulu. Doing so saved five to six minutes of flight time, which was critical in landing safely. We probably couldn't have stayed in the air for that much longer. With my experience, I already knew that I couldn't maintain altitude at 36,000 feet. To do that, I'd have had to bring the nose up, which in these circumstances would've made the plane stall and fall out of the sky. If I wanted to keep airspeed, I had to keep the nose down. I had to maintain the aerodynamic parameters that would keep the airplane flying. Thankfully, I managed to do that.

I also think back to a couple of years ago when I was flying a 757 to New York. We were 10 or 15 miles from the airport at 3,000 feet, and as I started turning left toward Liberty International Airport, runway 22L (left), we were hit by a Canada goose. It slammed right into my windshield. We were going about 290 miles per hour. It felt like somebody had shot the airplane with a 50-millimeter gun. The blood and guts of the goose covered the entire windshield, but it was more concentrated on my side. I couldn't see out. I told the copilot, "It's your aircraft." Thankfully, we managed to land safely.

Fate can sometimes lead you toward danger, but it can also ensure your survival. I don't think we realize just how many near misses we have in life. I firmly believe we are held in the Creator's hands. So many times, I've come to the very edge, when at any moment, something could snatch me away and I'd meet eternity.

❈ ❈ ❈

It's finally time for the call.

Separately, they ask us each 33 questions— first me, then Paul, then Ed.

In the end, they tell us that everything we told them was exactly as it was on the cockpit voice recorder. They already knew the answers. That is what tends to happen in scenarios like this. They tell us they'll continue their review and that they'll get back to us, but that, regarding our grounded status, we'll most likely be in the clear.

An ALPA rep calls and tells me that it's not only him on the phone. There's also an NTSB, FAA, and a United representative on the line. He tells me to not be concerned or worried—that they're all here to congratulate us and thank us for a job well done. The NTSB representative tells me, "Captain, you have no idea what a pleasure it is to be talking to a live pilot instead of picking up the pieces from the bottom of the ocean, putting them back together, and guessing what had happened." I will never forget these words. They told me that the investigation was going to continue and eventually someone from United's chief pilot's office would get back to us.

Once again, it is time to wait.

Chapter 20

1979

I enrolled in Sierra Academy of Aeronautics. Quickly, however, I began to realize that I had a problem. A major problem. There I was in school, but I had only enough money to do two or three flying lessons. I didn't have the money to even finish the private pilot courses, let alone instrument and commercial multiengine courses. When school began, I even had to sort out how to get to class. Thankfully, my roommate Ron Tom had an old moped in his garage and he told me that if I could get it working again it'd be mine. I knew about bikes from my motocross days, so I cleaned it up, put new spark plugs in, cleaned the carburetor, filled the bike up with gas, and I had my transportation. It was a joy to ride. It took me back to my motocross days in Iran. Sure, the speed maxed out at around 15 miles per hour, but it was mine.

I didn't care; my mind was set on mastery. The first step was ground school, and then you do your flight training. I needed to earn money. Ron Tom was kind enough to get me a job at his dad's store. It wasn't much, but it made a huge difference.

Whenever I was stressed during this early period in my flight training, I'd go running near the Oakland Airport. A park by the water had a jogging track. I'd run around there, watching big jets fly overhead. I loved it. I've always enjoyed running, and I was improving. I'd try to get high on running. I'd run until my body couldn't take it anymore. I wanted to be a pilot and I wanted to succeed. The question on my mind while running was how I was going to get enough money. I struggled to come up with ideas. I decided I'd focus on all my written tests, private, commercial, instrument, etc. It took a long time, but I had to finish. Until I had all the licenses, I couldn't get a serious job. Jumping ahead a bit—even when I was teaching ground school and they were paying me $8 an hour, it cost $150 per hour for flight instruction. I'd have to work 20 hours for one hour of flight instruction. So I was running a lot throughout this time to deal with the stress. I'd run until I'd throw up. There were many days I'd cry and ask for help from the man upstairs. I asked Him to show me different ways to do this because it just seemed like there was no hope, that there was no way to get this done. But no matter how hard it got, something inside me always said not to quit. Just keep doing this. Keep doing what you're doing. Things are going to turn around, just keep going. No matter how long I was running, whether it was one mile or five, no matter how tired I was, I'd made a promise to myself to sprint the last 300 yards. I'd kick into high gear and give it all I had. It was just me against myself. There was nobody else to please, nobody to impress.

A few times, however, there was this guy who'd come and watch me run. He was a scout for the San Francisco 49ers of the National Football League. He approached me after one of my running sessions. He thought my running was great and he suggested that I should consider being a wide receiver because of my height and how skinny I was. I was six-foot-two and weighed only 180 pounds. He told me that if I wanted to, I could come up to the training camp for the 49ers and give it a try. I didn't know much about American football at the time, but my passion was flying. I wanted to be a 747 pilot. Nothing else mattered. He could have offered me a top job on Wall Street or a perfect career as a movie star and I would have turned him down. My focus was singular, as was my passion. All my drive was geared toward becoming an airline pilot. No matter what. After all it took to even be able to run around this track to alleviate my stress (remember, I was once paralyzed from the neck down), I couldn't consider giving up this dream for anything. As you might have guessed, I turned him down.

Since, as previously mentioned, I didn't have enough money for the full instruction, I talked to the counselors and learned I could do all my academic training before even getting on an airplane, which is something I recommend to anyone financially challenged who's thinking of getting into aviation.

In ground school, you learn the basics of aviation before setting foot on a plane. You learn the preparations that must be done before you fly, and you have a chance to go up in the air with an instructor to get a feel for it before you start your flight training. Since I didn't have the money, I focused on that and on mastering each course: private, instrument, commercial, and airline transport. I invested my limited funds where and how I could. Ron Tom was always challenging and encouraging me. I studied 16 hours a day.

I finished a course in one year that normally took two and a half. I didn't have time to wait. I barely knew what I was going to eat the next day.

During one of the courses I was taking, Ron Tom told me that if I got 100 percent, he'd take me out to a steak dinner. I hadn't had a steak for more than four years.

Well, I got that 100, and we went out for steaks at a wonderful restaurant by the Oakland waterfront. Afterward, we went out to a club where I met a beautiful woman who looked like Princess Diana. She worked for Bank of America as a manager. I didn't know it then, but she'd be instrumental to my success, and she'd be my first girlfriend in the United States. It wasn't long before we started dating and moved in together. She was 19 and I was 21. Since she was a manager at Bank of America, she taught me how to build credit and get loans, which was key to my being able to afford aviation training. With interest, the $40,000 course ended up costing closer to $100,000, but I didn't care. For the first time, I had the ability to get the money to learn how to fly. This was the beginning of my path toward mastery in aviation.

In my mind, the pupil becomes the student, the student becomes the teacher, and the teacher becomes the master. During the coming years, I'd eat, sleep, drink, and speak aviation 18 hours a day. Nothing would stand in my way of becoming a 747 pilot for United.

❈ ❈ ❈

At the beginning of my aviation training, I became friends with two other Persian pilots. I thought we had something in common, but despite our quick friendship I soon learned we weren't the same. We were around the same age, but their parents supported them and gave them money. They didn't have to work for anything. They'd come and sit in a class for three or four hours, fly for one or two, and then have the whole afternoon or evening to go play and drink and party. I couldn't do that. I had to work full-time and fly in the evening any chance I got. For me, there was barely enough time in the day. I had nothing but the passion that they lacked. They wanted to have fun and party. Meanwhile, I was worried about what I was going to eat the next day and how I was going to afford to learn how to fly. I'd tell them that the path they were on was not congruent with wanting to become a commercial airline pilot. You simply cannot live that type of lifestyle when you're representing an airline. People's lives are in your hands. I told them that I couldn't be a part of the behavior they were up to. It was such an incredibly difficult decision to make. I desperately needed some connection to my past, but these guys weren't a good influence. I had to move myself and my friendship away from them and focus on flying.

There were other students from other countries. Some of these people, with work ethic like my erstwhile Persian friends, go off and become pilots. They get their commercial license with 250 hours and go back to their home country where they're put in the right seat of a 737 and they just hope that nothing ever goes wrong. Because if it did, they wouldn't be prepared. Mastery must be the goal if you want to become a pilot. People's lives depend on it.

❈ ❈ ❈

After finishing all the ground school classes, I took a course to become a ground school instructor. I passed and started teaching as an Advanced Ground Instructor, or AGI. Teaching allowed me to keep my foot in the door of aviation and to retain my visa status while providing me with an opportunity to learn and perfect my technical skills. I did this for around six months. I still had yet to fly.

My first student paid me with a 10-speed bike. Only five of the speeds worked. I was living in Hayward, near the Southland Mall with my girlfriend and I was taking the bus to and from class each day since I ended up selling the moped I'd repaired for a few hundred dollars. My daily budget was a dollar. I'd spend 50 cents on bus fare on the way to class and 50 cents back. If I decided to treat myself to a Coke that day, I'd have to walk home. So 10 hours of instruction got me a 10-speed bike that I was able to use to get to and from class. Many of my fellow students had come from rich families from places like Saudi Arabia. They'd show up to class in their fancy cars, driving Trans Ams and Porsches and Ferraris, and then there I was, their instructor, wheeling in on a bicycle. But it didn't matter how many fancy cars they had; their hearts weren't in it, and many of them took more time than normal to learn basic skills. I had one student who'd consistently miss class. Once, when I called to ask where he was, he told me that he was off partying in Vegas. When I told him that if he didn't show up, I wouldn't get paid, he offered to pay me anyway. Money was of no matter to these people, and it was scary to think that some of them might become pilots one day.

Even though I'd yet to begin flying consistently, I realized there were still opportunities to learn that I could take advantage of while saving up for flight lessons. I asked the instructors at the flight academy if I could sit in on in-air instruction and observe and learn. I wouldn't do anything but sit there and take notes. Soon after I got up there, I realized that the instructors were teaching the same thing over and over to their students. So I'd take my notepad with me and take notes on how to do the maneuvers. I'd be totally focused on what the instructor was teaching, because the student was doing the same thing I'd soon do. I was determined to get better and better by any means I could. I learned how the maneuvers felt, and how the plane handled. Up in the air with the students and instructors, I had the opportunity to sense it time and time again. If a student got scared practicing a maneuver, I'd get scared too. But I learned what to expect, and I grew more comfortable in these scenarios, so that by the time I was behind the controls I was already comfortable with what I had to do.

I even trained at home. I bought a poster of a Cessna 172, and with a few pieces of wood, I created the control column and pedals. I put the poster on my wall, and I'd visualize flying the airplane. I practically created my own simulator. I knew that if I simulated flying in my head, and if I gave life to it with my imagination, I could feel it, sense it, and learn, preparing myself for training in the cockpit. I was priming myself for getting behind the controls. I wanted to seize every opportunity I could grab. I wanted to master every aspect of aviation that I could. A quitter never wins, and a winner never quits. I'd keep going, no matter what.

Chapter 21

2018

It's about two months after the incident. I don't end up having to go back to training. Their hats are off to us, and they put me back on the line.

When I finally go back to work, the chief pilot asks me to come into his office. All the other flight managers are there. He introduces me to everyone: "You all heard about 1175. They had a catastrophic engine failure over the Pacific Ocean," he says. "Well, this is Captain Behnam, who was in command of the jet at the time." Then we walk out of his office, where all the other pilots are gathered, doing their paperwork before their flights. They roll in a cart with a cake on it, "1175" inscribed atop the icing. The chief pilot gives me the floor to speak.

I don't tell the whole story, but I take some questions.

Someone wants to know if the airplane really rolled and how I had to handle the rudders.

I tell them. I say thank you to everyone.

They give me a standing ovation. Gaining the respect of my peers is one of the most wonderful things to happen throughout this whole process. It's a lovely feeling.

Once I'm back at work, things fall into a routine. It's a bit different, but mainly the same. At work, I end up flying the same plane again to Honolulu. It gives me a moment of pause but it passes. I trust our mechanics and United's decision to return the jet to service. It flies without incident.

Kathi Hurst from ALPA calls me out of the blue one day in the spring of 2019. She tells me that they're nominating Ed, Paul, and me for the Superior Airmanship Award in recognition of our phenomenal work. This is huge news. ALPA has over 66,000 members, and the award has only previously been bestowed several times since the organization's inception. It's like the Oscars of aviation. We were just doing what we loved. We were doing our job, living our passion. That alone is reward enough, but to receive this honor on top of it is mind-blowing.

That July we all make the trek to ALPA's headquarters in Washington, D.C., for the awards ceremony. My children and girlfriend go with me. I'm blessed that they're by my side. There are 600 or 700 people there. They hand out all sorts of awards, including legislative awards, safety awards, and assistant awards. So much has happened since the flight.

We are introduced and given the award by Captain Joe DePete, the president of ALPA, and Captain Todd Insler, United's ALPA Master Executive Chairman, or MEC. They are stellar pilots and men. After receiving the award, I have the opportunity, and the immense honor, to share my gratitude with those in the room, with Ed, Paul, ALPA, United, and my family. This is what I say:

> **I'd like to extend my sincere thanks to everyone here at ALPA and for this incredible award! I am deeply touched by it and extremely grateful. It is an honor and privilege to be here this evening among you.**
>
> **To be recognized by your peers is an extraordinary blessing. I was also blessed to have two fine pilots in the cockpit with me on February 13, 2018. We were also blessed with a very capable crew onboard that day.**
>
> **Paul Ayers, Ed Gagarin, and the crew showed remarkable strength and courage during a terri-**

fying time. So I don't stand here alone this evening, but with those dear people who helped to bring Flight 1175 to Honolulu. It was indeed a team effort.

For the passengers onboard 1175, I express my gratitude for them, for they too possessed remarkable courage.

At the time of the incident, it felt like we had a midair collision. It was like hitting a brick wall at 560 miles per hour. No one knew if we would make it. No one knew if the plane was going to fall apart. No one knew if we would ever see our families again.

I have been an airline pilot for 32 years, but never experienced anything like that event. There was no training for it. When the instruments tell you a different story from what you're experiencing, and the flight conditions deteriorate, all you can do is your level best and fall back on what you know.

I prayed that day that God would help us land that 777 on the ground in Honolulu. I prayed that no one would be hurt. We all prayed. We are here today because our prayers were answered.

That in and of itself is a tremendous award. We were given another day to live.

So to be here this evening and to be recognized for our efforts is a humbling experience—one that I will never forget, nor cease to appreciate. I will always cherish it. With all my heart, I thank you!

The whole ceremony is poignant. Standing up there in front of my peers and receiving a standing ovation is such a great honor and privilege. To gain the respect of your fellow pilots means the world to me. I feel truly blessed to be alive in the company of such wonderful people, and to be a part of a union as wonderful as ALPA. In a way, during the speeches, we relive those 40 minutes. Our families and those in the audience who hear us talk about what happened, learn more details and experience the incident in a new way.

Although some pilots and United Airlines officials knew of the story, after the award ceremony, the news about the flight spreads. The people responsible for United Airlines pilot training begin to look to disseminate the word about the incident. I'm asked to give presentations about the event for them at civilian venues. My animation video is approved, and it becomes available to pilots during their training.

❋ ❋ ❋

Prior to the award, the media had begun to pay attention to me. Word got out that an Iranian American pilot had safely landed the plane. Since coming to America, I've struggled to find a connection to my past. In the early '80s, when I began my aviation career, there were hardly any Iranian pilots. Now there are maybe 50 of them working for United, Delta, and American, but their seniority is below mine, so there's little connection. I buried myself in my pursuit of aviation when I came to America. I became Americanized. For a long time, I had no family over here. But since landing Flight 1175, I was blessed with the chance to reach out again to the Iranian community both locally and through social media. I was embraced and began to get involved again in the culture. I'd done something that people in Iran are extremely proud of, and I was welcomed.

I intend to take this platform I've been gifted with and motivate people to thrive in their lives—to work hard, empower themselves, and reach the greatness they were all created with. I've been given the chance to be a father figure, a guiding and helping hand to others, the way my father was to me. I want to give people hope and peace. I want them to succeed as I have. Right now, there are people with master's degrees on the side of the street with no work, no job prospects, and no future. There are fathers ashamed that they can't buy food for their families. There are factory workers who if they go on strike could be put in prison just for asking for their rights.

People must have the right to speak their minds and to be heard. We will never get past our considerable differences by breeding hatred and enacting violence. Evil begets evil. It never breeds good. Each one of us is responsible for our actions. Each one of us has the responsibility to contribute good to society.

Currently we're seeing people stuck in the past, tethered by generational hatred and bigotry. That tether is strong, but it's not impervious to change. It may take a great deal of work to break that tether, but with education, patience, and charity, those constraints will be broken, and peace will be attainable. Any change in society is ignited by individual actions that can turn society toward good or evil. It's our choice. We are free to choose. But will we? We must choose to move society toward good.

❋ ❋ ❋

After the award, interviews continue and speaking engagements multiply. The more people I motivate, the more I'm motivated to better myself and grow. The fact that I can stand in front of hundreds of airline employees, managers, COOs, CFOs, and CEOs and talk about my experience of overcoming adversity in a language that's not even my native tongue is powerful for me, but also for others who are afraid they might not be able to overcome the odds. You can. And you will. It's possible to come from thousands of miles away in the Middle East from a different culture and find success in this wonderful country—in this wonderful world. It takes time to adjust and adapt, to learn a new language and become a part of a new society, to go to school, to not have the money to go after the dream and to figure out how to live on a dollar a day, while giving up on a relationship because I knew that my love for aviation was bigger. If I'd given up in any of these cases, in my near-death experiences or doubts—anything—I wouldn't be here to tell my story, and neither would 380 other people be alive to tell theirs.

❈ ❈ ❈

Social media opens things up for me. I can communicate across the world. I've learned that I breathe hope into my followers. I listen to what they say. I see them find their own voices. It's wonderful to see this happening. Women are becoming more courageous, and men have reached out to me to tell me that thanks to messages I've shared, they've given up on drugs, or they've moved away from suicidal ideations. They've shown me that there's good in this world, and that people want leadership. They want change, and they're willing to risk their lives to get there. I feel blessed to know that I've been able to impact these people's lives for the better and that I'm able to continue to do so.

We all have a role to play, whether we know it or not. I believe that there is a purpose and reason for why we are all on this Earth. Whether it's significant or not, whether it's big or small, it all makes a difference. There's a defining moment in everyone's life. I believe that those 40 minutes in the air were the defining moments in mine. I played a part in avoiding what would have been one of the worst aviation disasters in history. I was able to avoid death. It's my mission now to encourage others—to become a leader, to help people, whether old or young, Black or white, Muslim or Christian, to go after their goals and dreams and to realize their true potential. I want to help them become the giant that they were created to be and to help them make a difference in this world.

Chapter 22

1980

In my opinion, a "pilot" is a person who pushes a barge down the Mississippi River. But to be an *aviator*, you need to be trained to be an aviator. I am an aviator. As I touched on earlier, it wasn't uncommon for people to come to the United States from abroad to study aviation at schools in Napa or the Bay Area or Sacramento. They'd come to the U.S., train at a flight academy, get their private, instrument, and commercial certification, and then go back home and start flying jets. But many of these pilots don't have adequate experience. They don't actually have what is required for their job. That's why you'll sometimes see crashes in other parts of the world. Yes, the systems on airplanes are incredibly good, and many pilots go their entire careers without anything bad happening. But just hoping for the best is no way to be an airline pilot. You must be prepared for the worst-case scenario. You must have the aeronautical knowledge and the foundation to handle any situation. That was my goal when I set out to master aviation. I'd go after any way I could to increase my hours in the air, whether I was flying, instructing, or simply observing. I'd be in the air whenever I could.

I eventually saved up enough money teaching ground school to begin my flight training. It was such an amazing feeling to finally take to the air. All my hard work and visualization paid off. I worked my way from private, instrument, commercial, and then to multi-engine instruction. I was a quick learner. The average person took 10 hours of flight time for multi-engine training. I did it in two, because I'd already logged nearly 15 hours in the back seat observing the instructor with other students. I tell anybody who wants to fly to not even get in the cockpit until they've memorized all the profiles, because up in the air you won't have time to think about these things. By profiles, I mean takeoff, landing, approach … all the different segments of flying and the procedures that apply. Basically, how to fly an airplane in myriad situations. You have to know them by memory, because once you're in the cockpit, there's no time to react. All the hours I spent in the back seat flying were like a simulator for me.

I'd practiced all the moves already in my head, so when I was in an airplane, I never had to think about them.

I passed all my courses as quickly as I could and became a flight instructor. It meant even more hours for my logbook and an opportunity for more money to help make ends meet. Teaching students to fly and sharing my passion for flight made the job so incredibly rewarding. As a flight instructor, I met all kinds of people—people of all kinds of dispositions and personalities. Each student brought with them their dreams, their goals, and certainly their fears. Flying takes courage, and flight training can make a person keenly aware of their fears and limitations. Someone might freak out on the spot or make an accidental steep turn, and the instructor might have to take over. I had to deal with such instances several times during my teaching career.

One of my early students was on the way to becoming a very good pilot. He had the makings, and I thought he had the desire. We were working through his training, and one day it came time for him to practice spin recovery. That is when the plane is purposely placed into a spin and the student must recover and regain straight and level flight. Spins can be extremely dangerous. A certain mindset is required to go through this process. A student must understand and believe in the principles of aerodynamics. They must understand the forces acting upon their plane and what it takes to equalize those forces to achieve straight and level flight. I had my student go through the checklist. We were at a sufficient altitude. We'd flown to the training area, where we were assured that there wasn't a large population below, or obstacles that would come into play.

Next, the student checked the doors of the plane to make sure they were shut and that the seatbelts were secure. Check. The student checked to make sure the fuel valve switch was on. Check. The fuel mixture had to be set to rich. Check. The gauges were indicating normal levels and temperatures. Check. The carburetor heat was set to hot. Check. Magneto switches were set to "both." Check. The student performed a gentle S-turn. He made a 15-degree bank to the left and then to the right, checking for traffic below. The airspace was free from traffic.

To enter the spin, the student induced a stall. He pulled back on the throttle, raising the nose of the plane. Then the student stepped on the left rudder pedal to put the plane into a spin.

The plane went into a full autorotation.

Things were going according to the lesson—until the student panicked.

Now, to recover from a spin, it's necessary to pull the throttle all the way back to full idle and to step on the opposite rudder pedal from the direction of the spin. Pushing forward on the control column breaks the stall. But the student froze. His hands froze on the controls, and he couldn't let go.

This was a huge problem. I needed to get control of the plane away from the frightened student. His fear kept him from thinking clearly and acting appropriately. We were losing altitude quickly. The recovery maneuver is not difficult, but you must follow the correct steps in the correct order. I managed to get control and we did recover from the spin, but the ground was very close. By the time we recovered, we were at 1,500 feet with not much room to spare.

We often lose sight of our own difficulties, forgetting the rudiments that get us safely from point A to Z. Fear gets in our way and paralyzes us. This can be deadly, as I learned that day with my student. Seeing fear first-hand as a flight instructor, I've learned to help people work through fear by using knowledge and science. It's not surprising that gravitational pull and spinning can disorient us, but it's important to remember that we can easily recover homeostasis and straight and level flight by bringing lift, thrust, drag, and weight into equality. It's all about balance and finding your center. When we allow circumstances to push us out of our center, we become agitated. We abandon reason. We spiral out of control. Whether you're flying or on the ground, keeping forces in check will make for a smoother journey to your destination and to your success. I don't know whether this student of mine ever got beyond his fears and advanced in aviation. But fear got the better of him that day, and that it stopped him from achieving his goals. Fear of the unknown can keep us hostage and keep our goals out of reach.

❈ ❈ ❈

My first nonteaching job after finishing flight school was flying canceled checks for First Interstate Bank from Hayward, California, north to Marin County. I took this job because I wanted to make sure I had different kinds of experience in my logbook—charter work, corporate jobs—other than just as a flight instructor.

I'd get up at four and leave Hayward at six in the morning to fly to Marin County in a single-engine cargo plane. Once I arrived, I had a bunch of downtime. I didn't want to lose a single minute of the day. After several trips, it occurred to me that I could be using this time to my advantage by teaching students in Marin County. This would put even more hours in my logbook. I talked to the school at the airport and they gave me a couple of students. I'd spend my downtime flying with those students, and then at five, I'd hop back on the same plane, park it in Hayward, and fly with my other students there until about nine at night. Then I'd come home and start everything over again the next morning.

By doing this I was able to be more productive and make some extra money, but I still wasn't getting the hours I needed. I had my eyes set on a commuter airline based in Chico called West Air. I kept sending them résumé after résumé, whenever I had a reasonable amount of flight time to add. Time and time again they'd tell me I didn't have enough hours, that I didn't have enough twin-engine or Cessna 402 time.

I kept flying. One evening in Hayward on one of my trips, I saw a Cessna 402 come in as I was getting gas at the station. For me at the time, this was a huge airplane. It was a twin-engine, way fancier and bigger than the plane I was currently flying. This plane landed at the airport on a regular basis and the same pilot was always behind the controls. I befriended him. His name was Steve. I asked him what he did, and he told me he was a cargo pilot for a Part 135 outfit. He told me he flew for this outfit out of Reno, Nevada, and that they had flights to Las Vegas and Seattle as part of their daily route. This sounded incredible. All I could think about were the hours I could build up by flying the twin.

I said, "That's wonderful! That's my dream. I want to fly 402s that fly cargo."

Over time, we built a rapport. One day I asked him if he'd kindly pass my résumé on to the chief pilot in case he needed to hire another pilot.

He said, "Sure thing. No problem."

I felt great. My résumé was in great shape, as I'd been updating it and sending it out as often as I could, and I felt confident that I'd hear from the owner.

I started seeing Steve three or four nights a week. We would chat a bit, and every couple of months I'd give him a new résumé with more hours, since I was flying almost 100 hours a month. He'd graciously accept, but said the chief pilot wasn't hiring anybody at the time.

Time passed, and I didn't even get a no, which wasn't uncommon. I'd sent several hundred résumés out in the past month and hadn't heard back from a single one, so when I heard no news from Steve, I didn't think anything of it. I kept flying the canceled checks every day, getting up at four, teaching in Marin County, and flying back to Hayward.

One day, I noticed that Steve wasn't flying the cargo plane. Another man had taken his place. I went over and introduced myself and told him that I knew about their airplane and route, that they flew from Hayward to Reno, and then Reno to Las Vegas, Vegas to Reno, then back to Hayward, and then Seattle and back. The oils never got cool on that plane. It was always running. I asked the new guy where Steve was.

He said, "Oh, Steve? Steve's no longer with us."

I asked him who he was.

I was talking to the chief pilot and owner, which was fantastic. I told him, "That's great! Because I've been giving Steve my résumés to give to the chief pilot—and that's you. Have you seen any of them?"

He hadn't. I couldn't believe it. Steve had never passed on a single résumé. He was busy worrying about his own job, which he ended up losing. The good news was that the chief pilot and I had an immediate rapport. My enthusiasm inspired me to ask the owner if he was hiring. He was. I had a copy of my résumé on hand and gave it to him. He looked it over for a bit and asked if I was busy. I wasn't. He asked me to hop on the plane. He said, "We're flying to Reno."

"Just like that?" I asked.

"Just like that," he said. "I'll show you all the way up to Reno how to operate this airplane."

"What about ground school?" I asked.

"We'll do it in the air."

I canceled my student for that night, and we hopped on the plane.

It was my first time flying a plane like this. It was like going from driving a Prius to a bus. The basics are the same, but if you've never been behind the wheel of a bus, it takes some getting used to.

He told me, "I don't care what you have to do. You just need to make sure this cargo gets to Reno on time."

We flew 500 feet over I-80 all the way through the mountains to Reno. He dimmed the lights for me to see the edge of the mountains and to stay "on" the freeway.

"This airplane has to come in overnight," he continued. "You're going to be on this job five days a week. The airplane lands in Hayward. It's your plane, and you've got to fly to Reno and back."

Once we landed in Reno, the job was mine. My patience, persistence, and perseverance paid off. He then told me that I'd have to fly back to Hayward at one in the morning. I wasn't done yet. I had more work to do.

Chapter 23

2018

I almost die again. It's April 16, a few months after the incident, which was on February 13. I'd gone back to work, and, of course, my first flight is to Honolulu. The flight goes well, but when I land, I begin to feel sick.

I come down with borderline pneumonia and bronchitis from time to time. I figure it might also be the stress of it all. The changing weather patterns between California and Hawaii likely don't help. Regardless, I have a fever and a cold, and I hole myself up in my hotel room. I'm unfortunately unable to enjoy the beauty of the island. I accept that I'm going to be stuck here for a good 10 days or so.

At the same time, my daughter Emma is on her way to the Big Island of Hawaii to go to school. She's going to be studying marine biology at the University of Hawaii at

Hilo. I fly out to meet her and my girlfriend, Maleah, but I'm still not feeling nearly as good as I thought I would. I'm just barely present. It's a miserable handful of days. I just can't shake it. After a few more days in Hilo, Maleah and I fly back to San Francisco.

From the airport, we're driving our separate cars home, chatting on the phone. As we get close to Sacramento, around one in the morning, she takes the exit toward her house. My exit is still 30 minutes farther north. I continue along the freeway, trying my best to stay focused and awake.

I'm nearly home.

I'm driving and driving, but I feel something is off. The part of the freeway I'm on doesn't feel familiar to me. My eyes are heavy.

Did I miss my exit?

My right tire blows.

The car veers to the left. I hit the concrete median.

The car goes to the right. It feels like it might somersault and start rolling at over 65 miles per hour. I decide not to fight it. I let go of the controls. This prevents the car from skidding and rolling.

I hit the median head-on and the car rolls back, turns, and mercifully stops, facing the oncoming cars.

Chapter 23

I'm exhausted.

Moments before, I could barely keep my eyes open, but at least now I'm awake.

I hear a woman's voice, but I'm not sure from where.

I think I'm dead.

I turn to the left and right. There's nobody at the windows.

The voice is asking: "Are you okay? Are you okay? Are you okay?"

As my senses gradually return to me, I realize where it's coming from. It's one of those automated systems that alert someone that your car has crashed. Something had come up on the radar screen. With the voice located, I begin to realize where I am: in the middle of the freeway.

Cars are coming at me. My lights shoot out, head on into the oncoming traffic, cutting a hole through the night. In front of me, I can see lights. They come closer. They get bigger and brighter and then they turn. They go around me and pass.

I'm a sitting duck in the middle of the freeway. Cars continue to pass. I try to get out of the car, but I can't. I try again. I jiggle the door. It's jammed. I undo my seat belt and position myself with my legs facing the passenger side door. I kick it out and climb from the wreck.

An 18-wheeler comes at me from the darkness of the night. The driver slams on his brakes. The truck jackknifes and stops maybe 10 or 15 feet from my car. Thankfully, his position blocks all four lanes and any oncoming traffic. I'm safe from that at least. No one else is going to hit me.

The police show up. A passerby took care of calling the cops.

The police ask if I'm okay. I tell them I am, which likely paints a strange sight given I'm standing next to a destroyed car. But even though I feel okay, they tell me they're going to take me to the emergency room.

At the hospital, they check me over. I'm a bit injured from the seatbelt and have a little chest pain, but no broken bones, not even a broken finger. They're amazed that nothing more severe happened to me. I should be dead, or at the very least have some internal injuries.

I call Maleah and let her know what happened. She's in tears. She drives up to the hospital. After a little while longer, they discharge me, and Maleah takes me home. The next day I go to the gas station where my car had been towed.

They never really figure out why the tire exploded. They think that maybe I'd hit a sharp object on the freeway, maybe a bolt or a piece of metal. I'm incredibly lucky that the engine dampened the severity of the accident, as I'd hit the median perfectly head-on. The engine took the hardest hit—it fell through the bottom of the car. This, along with the seat belt and front and side airbags, ended up saving me. It really was a miracle. This experience reaffirms my belief that I'm here for something big, and that it's not yet my time.

Chapter 24

1983

I was balancing three jobs at this point. I'd get up in the morning and at six I'd fly to Marin County carrying bounced and canceled checks. Once I was there, I'd fly with my students, and when it was time to leave, I'd fly back to Hayward, have a quick sandwich, and fly with my other students until about 9:30 at night. Then at 10 I'd hop on the twin-engine to Reno. I'd get there at 11 or so and catch a nap on a couch in the Fixed Base Operator (FBO) office that I shared with a dog. The plane would then go to Las Vegas and back. Then, at one in the morning, I'd fly back to Hayward, go home, sleep for two hours or so, take a shower, and go back to the airport at 5:30 to take flight again at six.

I was determined to make it work and build my hours, never losing sight of my goal of flying for United Airlines as a 747 pilot. I would not relent. I refused to settle for less. I would not give up. I kept using visualization. I'd picture myself in the cockpit of a 747. Daily, I'd see myself achieving my goals. It's important to keep the vision alive to make it a reality.

I kept flying. I kept imagining. And each day I came closer to what I wanted. Having and creating positive thoughts is essential. There was, of course, fatigue during times of little progress. There will be difficulties, but you must remember to keep the positive energy flowing. Discouragement is the enemy, and you cannot let it linger. You must push it aside and keep going.

As I mentioned, during all of this I was still teaching ground school and teaching people how to fly. Teaching was then and still is a passion of mine. Regardless of your profession, it is critical to know as much as you can, so that when difficult situations occur, you know how to handle them. Knowing how to operate under stress is, in flying, like knowing our aircraft profiles. You must know what you might be up against. You need to know the facts, and you need to have them ready.

Knowing profiles was essential for me when I was flying the Reno to Las Vegas route. The plane had no radar. Ice would build up on the windows, and because of the mountains, I had to climb above 11,000 feet with no oxygen mask (you can stay above 10,000 feet for 30 minutes) and then quickly descend. At times, the flying was treacherous, but through this experience, I became a better aviator.

This extra experience was particularly useful when teaching. One of my students was a rugby player. He was a strong guy. We were working through his maneuvers. We'd done the steep turn and the stalls. He was getting ready for his check ride and spin demo and spin recovery.

When I was learning to fly, I had an aerobatic instructor who'd tell stories about pushing the airplane, where you're not just doing turns at 20 or 30 degrees, but where you're tumbling the plane. You're doing loops and barrel rolls in a Cessna 150. I made sure to incorporate this in my flight training—because should an airplane get away from you, you must be able to control it. It's unfortunate that many pilots have never done stalls or spins. A lot of instructors won't teach it. They're dangerous maneuvers. One mistake and you're dead. But I wanted to learn these aerobatics, not only in case I found myself in a situation I needed to pull out of, but also because I wanted to become acclimated to operating an airplane under tremendous adverse effects, such as being upside down or at a 60- or 90-degree bank.

My instructor's name was Art Smith. He taught me how

to become a good instructor and aerobatic pilot. He also taught night flying. He'd cover the six basic engine instruments with suction cups, and he'd tell me to feel the airplane, to fly it by sound. If I was to bring the nose up by five degrees, I was to visualize it and keep that angle. I didn't need to look at the instruments. If you're going 100 miles per hour and your hand is on the power control and you push your finger out, take note of how much you press the control forward. He'd ask me if I was at 100 miles per hour. He'd remove the cover and I'd be right at 100. I had such a deep thirst for knowledge and such a desire to become better than my instructors that, over the years, my skills would surpass Art's. But 10 years later, once I'd begun flying jets, he was still a flight instructor, and he was looking to leave his job. I remembered him and I brought him to United and he got hired. I was proud and glad that I was able to bring things full circle and help someone who'd helped me so much.

Now I was teaching spins and spin recovery to this rugby player, and I was sitting in the right seat with my hands folded. Art had taught me that the best instructor in the world is the one who can guide and talk to the student very calmly and tell them what to do without touching the controls—trusting the student enough that they could do exactly what the instructor says and recover from a very bad situation. With my student flying the plane, we started to go into a spin maneuver.

Spins basically occur when you stall the airplane and don't have enough foot pressure on the rudder during the stall. Since there's not enough pressure on the rudder, the wing drops first, and the aircraft spins. Rather than the nose falling forward, the plane goes into a bank and starts spinning out of the air and tumbling and coming down to the ground.

We'd practice these by doing three turns. We would start out at 3,500 feet, and each turn lose 300 or 500 feet. Normally after three turns, I'd tell the student to relax. I'd tell them not to pull back on the control, but rather to push the nose forward and kick the opposite rudder to stop the turn, making the plane go into a nosedive that they would pull out of and bring the plane back up. But this time, when the airplane began to spin, the rugby player got scared. He froze up on the controls.

We went through one spin.

Two spins.

Three spins.

I said, "Okay, Push the nose over, level the wings. Relax. Pressure on the control."

You can't be tense in these situations. If you pull back too fast, you can rip the wings off the airplane.

We were still spinning, and he was still frozen. He wouldn't let go.

We were on the fourth spin.

The fifth.

The ground approached. We'd lost almost 2,000 feet. We only had 1,500 feet left before hitting the ground.

He still wasn't letting go. His body and brain just shut down due to the stress and shock. He gazed at the ground as if he wanted to see his own death. I had to get my hands on the controls. Someone had to push the nose down to make the plane flyable, but he kept pulling it up, thinking he was going to prevent the airplane from falling to the ground. My martial arts training came to mind. There's a maneuver in karate called enpi, an elbow strike to someone's ribs. I do that and knock the wind out of him. He let go of the controls. By the time I recovered the plane, we were 900 feet off the ground. I was able to bring the nose up gently and smoothly with only 500 feet left. We had both almost died. But I remained calm and focused. I knew how to fly in adverse circumstances. It's experiences like these that equipped me to handle Flight 1175 on that fateful day.

❋ ❋ ❋

Balancing three jobs and teaching was certainly not my end goal. I was flying to build up hours. I had my eyes set on a commuter airline called West Air. Their headquarters was in Chico. I'd been sending my résumé to them for quite some time with no response. One of my days off was on a day that I heard West Air was interviewing, so I drove up to Chico with my résumé in hand. I was determined to get the job. I knew a couple of people who'd been hired by West Air, so I knew where the chief pilot's office was. I got there early, at seven in the morning. He wasn't there yet, so I sat down and waited.

When he arrived at eight, I introduced myself. I said, "Sir, my name is Christopher." I got into my background a bit and continued, "I've been sending you résumés, and I'd love to work for your company."

He asked me if I had an interview scheduled for that day. I didn't and I told him as such. "No, I don't have an interview, but I just wanted to come and introduce myself, and shake your hand so you can put a face to my name. But whenever you do decide to hire somebody, please let me know."

He paused for a moment and said, "Well, why don't you hang around. Let me see what happens."

I did that. I sat in the lobby and waited. His schedule was jammed. People interviewing came in and out of his office all day, but I still waited. I didn't even go to the bathroom. I didn't want to risk missing the one chance he might come out looking to speak to me. Finally, at five in the evening, after seeing a handful of candidates throughout the day, he came out and looked at me with amazement and said, "You're still here."

"Yes, sir," I said. I'd waited for nine hours.

"Why?"

And I told him why. "You told me to wait, so I did."

He invited me to his office, and we had a brief meeting. He was impressed I'd hung around all day for the job, and he hired me on the spot. He told me that school would start in two weeks in the right seat of a 10-seat Cessna 402. I was absolutely delighted. I had one more rung on the ladder of my journey toward mastery of aviation and the cockpit of a 747.

I went back home and told my girlfriend everything that was going on. She was happy for me, but unfortunately this would eventually also spell the end of our relationship. She'd come to visit me in Chico for a while, but she wanted to live in San Francisco and that wasn't something I was able to provide.

❋ ❋ ❋

When I first got the job at West Air, my only means of

transportation was a dune buggy I'd purchased for $250. It rained the entire way up to Chico. The buggy had no roof, and the spark plugs kept getting wet and the car would quit on me. But I didn't care. I was living my dream and I had my whole life in two suitcases in the back of that car. I got to Chico and took out a room in a Motel 6. Back then, it was still only $6 a night.

At the time West Air had 48 pilots, with me as the newest hire. I started ground school and did well. I moved on to flight training and did great at that too. Soon I became a pilot and started flying. I rented an apartment nearby with two other guys. Shortly after that was when my relationship finally ended. When it did, I dug even deeper into aviation. I started flying 80 to 100 hours each month to build up twin-engine time. I was working like crazy for about $8 an hour. Financially, I was going backward, making a third of what I had been making, but I didn't care. I needed to get more time so that I could be hired by the major airlines. That was the name of the game: Get the hours to stand out from the pack.

I enjoyed flying for West Air. I made some wonderful friends. Each day I was moving closer to my goal. But it wasn't always pure sunshine. Once, I was flying as a copilot from Sacramento International to Chico. The captain was in the right seat doing communication and navigation. We took off. We followed our checklists. At about

600 feet above the ground, he dropped his pen that he was using to take notes and write down frequencies from our communications with air traffic control. He ducked down to pick it up and we got hit by a bird head-on. We were in a small airplane, a 10-seat Cessna 402, and the bird went right through the windshield, scraped the top of the captain's head, and continued into the cabin.

We heard a scream behind us. The bird had hit a passenger in the face. There were feathers and blood everywhere. It was utter chaos. The wind was deafening. I knew that the first thing I had to do was focus on flying. If I didn't, we could lose everyone on board. I let the tower know what was happening. We declared an emergency and I made a left turn to land.

When we reached the gate, ambulances were at the ready. Paramedics took the passenger off the airplane. We never learned what exactly happened to the poor man, but we had done all we could. We contacted West Air and told them what happened. They sent a mechanic to fix the windshield, and the plane was ferried and flown to our maintenance facility in Fresno.

❋ ❋ ❋

I kept flying. In the early 1980s, no major airlines such as American, Delta, and United were hiring. There were so many pilots looking for jobs. If you wanted a pilot with blonde hair, blue eyes, and 10,000 hours, you could find one. Thousands of people who had a lot more flight time than I had were looking for these jobs. I was sending résumés to airlines over the world, but I wasn't getting any responses. West Air closed their base in Chico, and I followed them, and my dream, to Fresno. I would have followed them anywhere.

During this time, I met the woman who would become my wife. I frequently visualized the type of person I wanted to marry, down to every last detail. I told myself that when that person came into my life, I'd know she was the one. The first time we spoke, I would know. I could tell right from the get-go that she liked me—that we'd get married and have four kids — two girls and two boys. I set my mind to it, and that's exactly what happened.

But first I needed to talk to her.

I first met Beth in Fresno, California. She was a customer service agent for West Air. I was the captain of a Short 360, a 36-passenger commuter aircraft—a turboprop plane with a flight attendant. I was heading to my plane one day when I saw this beautiful blonde woman with curly hair. I knew she was the one. Summers in Fresno are hot, so I'd used that as an excuse to get to know her and check her out. I got off the plane and walked to the terminal, declaring that it was too hot to do paperwork outside. Beth had just finished her degree at Colgate University in Upstate New York and was working a summer job before going to San Diego to start her master's program. We started talking. I found out that my flight ended around the time she got off, so I made a habit of hanging around and we'd talk. After three or four weeks, I asked her to go for a walk and to have a coffee. She said yes and we started dating. On the third date, I confidently told her that I felt that she was going to fall in love with me and marry me and that we were going to have four kids.

She responded with an unsurprising, "Oh, really?" And that's how our relationship began.

I'd told her of my ambitions and my dream to fly a 747 for United. With her help, every month we sent résumés to almost 300 airlines in the United States, Africa, the Middle East, and Asia. The first 300 went out and we didn't get a single response. I wasn't even good enough for a no.

I flew more. I logged more hours. We updated my résumé, and she helped me send out 300 more.

The second month: nothing.

After the third month, we got a few no thank-yous. I still wasn't qualified enough, but this told me I was on the right track. A no was better than nothing. With each no I heard, the more I knew I'd eventually hear a yes. I kept flying, and eventually I got a request to interview with United. My dream was within reach. The dream that had been ignited when I was a child in Iran watching the Pan Am 747 take off.

Having a passion, a drive, that fire in your belly, is so important. Two things, I believe, are required to make a person successful: the *how* and the *why*. The *how* is everywhere around us. How do I drive a car? How do I become a millionaire? How do I become a pilot? But none of that matters if you do not understand your *why*—why you want to do something. You must understand that if you want to find your path. Once you understand your *why*, the *how* will reveal itself. If your dream is big enough, and you can see and visualize it in your mind's eye, you can know it's possible. However, once you visualize it in your mind, and it goes from your head to your heart, you begin to believe it. After it goes from your heart to your gut, it becomes a passionate, burning desire, to which you say, "I don't care what it takes. I'll do it." It's only then, through taking massive action, that one's dream becomes a reality. It won't happen on its own. If you can visualize it in your mind's eye, it is possible. If your *why* is big enough, the *how* will reveal itself.

Chapter 25

1985

I'd been sending out nearly 300 applications every three months with my updated hours. I was flying 80 to 100 extra hours a month. Eventually I got a few nos. Finally, I was invited to interview with Delta, American, Continental, United, Pan Am, Eastern, and TWA.

But my sights were on United. There were 16,000 applicants to United. I was one of them, and that was the only interview I took. I was going to make my dream a reality. I went to the interview. I was hired. And within a week, I was fired for not crossing the picket line.

As I said earlier, there was a strike going on in June of 1985 when I was called in for an interview. United fired everybody and was planning on rebuilding the airline with scabs. A few friends of mine had already been hired by United, so I picked their brains. I wanted to know what was going on with the strike. There had been a lot of mixed messages coming from ALPA. One week they'd tell you not to even go in and interview, and the next they'd say that it was okay to interview but that we shouldn't start classes. Sometimes we were told to go to school, but not to do our IOE—Initial Operating Experience—where you train to become a full-fledged pilot.

Despite the confusion, I eventually went in for an interview. The process took several days. I remember sitting there with Air Force and Navy pilots. At times, my mind drifted to the idea that I didn't stand a chance, but then I knew my resolve and interest would make all the difference. I heard some of them talking about going to work for Delta or American Airlines if this didn't work out, because they didn't have labor-management problems. But I wanted to be a United Airlines captain—nothing else would come close. I knew I would never be happy working for another airline; plus neither American nor Delta had 747s.

The interviews were rigorous. If you passed the first round by taking a written test, then you moved on to a medical test. They gave us this orange drink that served as part of a stress test. It makes your body shake and tremor. We were given the MMPI, or Minnesota Multiphasic Personality Inventory, that assesses our personality traits. Then we had to go on the flight simulator on a jumbo 767. I'd never been in a cockpit of that size. After the interview and testing, we all returned to Cherry Creek Hotel in Denver. The hotel has an old-fashioned front desk, behind which were slots for each room's mail. Everyone who had been interviewing had an envelope in their slot. If you had a white envelope, you had made it to the next step. If you had a brown envelope, you were washed out. You could feel the tension in the room. People's dreams were on the line. I waited for everyone to get their envelope. Then I walked to my box with my eyes closed. I'd memorized the way to it. I took the envelope and held it in my hands. My eyes were still closed. I felt the weight of my future in each breath.

I opened my eyes.

White.

I'd made it to the next round, where I'd interview with a captain and a person from human resources. In the interview, I remember being asked, "Why should I hire you? You're coming from a different country, and we have all these qualified pilots here in this country."

I told him that nobody was more enthusiastic about this opportunity than I was. I told him that it had been a dream of mine to fly a 747 for United since I was nine years old. I told him that I came from a different country with no money in my pocket, that I'd never done anything illegal, that I'd flown everything I could so I could build up the flight time. I told them about how I held three jobs at once, all for the one opportunity to sit in front of them and share my story.

I told him that I knew that they were hiring me not only as a flight engineer but also as someone who would eventually become a captain. I promised them that if they hired me, I would become the best captain United has ever known, not knowing that 35 years down the road, I would have the opportunity to prove it.

I went back to California. They were going to notify us by mail. Every day I checked. Every day my heart was racing. Finally the mail came. I had Beth go and open it. I couldn't bear the suspense. She took the envelope and slowly ripped it open. She took out the letter inside and read it. She looked at me.

"What?"

She smiled. "You got the job."

It wasn't just her smiling at me that day—it was the whole world. Here was this kid who was born in a small village in Iran, got out of the country to England while not speaking a word of English, who made his way, essentially penniless, to the United States—and now had landed his dream.

United got moving right away. They contacted me and told me that I'd be starting school the next week. But the strike was still going on. I contacted ALPA. They told me not to go to school and not to break the strike. My father, being part of the labor movement, taught me the value of helping the underdog and not taking food off somebody else's table. I'd stand in solidarity with the strike. I called United and asked them if I could have two or three weeks to give West Air some time.

But United fired me. I watched my dream disappear. But I could not be a strikebreaker. To be one would not have aligned with my value system and integrity.

The problem was, though, that I'd already quit my job at West Air. I'd achieved my dream and lost it.

I pushed on. I called up West Air and asked for my old job back. They said they could give it to me, but I'd have to start at the bottom of the seniority list. I went from number 10 to number 500. I was on reserve. There were no schedules. I did this for a few months before realizing it was no longer a home for me. I couldn't grow any longer. I left West Air and got hired by Evergreen International, a cargo airline. I'd be flying in the right seat of a 727. Evergreen was a small company, a subcontractor to UPS. I stuck around on that job for six months before leaving.

Deep down I knew I'd never be happy flying for anyone other than United. I'd never be happy flying for American Airlines. They didn't have 747s, and my goal was specific. I had no interest in just being a pilot. Everything that came my way was going to be a stepping stone to flying a 747 for United. You're going to climb the ladder of life no matter what, even if you don't try, so you must be decisive in the path you choose. You must be precise. You don't want to climb a ladder, reach the top, and realize it was leaning against the wrong wall the entire time. If you don't follow your heart, your passion will be aimless as will your progress. But it bears repeating: If you follow your *why*, the *how* will follow.

ALPA sued United and after two or three months of negotiation they came around to an agreement. United had to give jobs back to everybody, though new pilots would come in on B-scale, meaning they'd get paid less. Even though United started taking pilots back, it took them two years to call me back to interview again. I had to go through a reselection process of testing and interviews. Luckily I passed, and on March 16, 1987, I finally became a full-fledged pilot for United, flying a 727 as a flight engineer.

❈ ❈ ❈

When people become pilots for United, they're usually

surrounded by their family and friends, and it's a joyous occasion. There were about 30 of us in my graduating class. Everybody had a family member, a boyfriend, or girlfriend present, but I had nobody. I had nobody to pin my wings on my shirt. It was a very sad feeling. Since arriving in the United States, I was primarily by myself, apart from Ron Tom taking me out for that delicious steak dinner. I had no family in the country. Nobody to say, "Good job," or "I'm proud of you." I had nobody to go through the pain or the excitement for all of this with me. It was very difficult to be a stranger in a country that was in a cold war with the country of my birth, while wonderful, innocent diplomats had been taken as hostages. I was amazed at the culture of United Airlines—that no one, not once, ever looked down on me or looked at me differently because of my national heritage. I am indebted to this wonderful company for the opportunity of my career.

Toward the end of the Shah's regime in 1979, he tried to amend things with the opposition. My father was part of that opposition, and the Shah's government sent him to become the Iranian ambassador to Spain. My family lived in the embassy compound in Madrid. It looked like a miniature White House. There were two buildings, a second next to the mini White House, which was my dad's office. They also had residences where the ambassadors lived. It was all very nice. It gave off the energy of some fancy neighborhood like Martha's Vineyard or Nantucket. However, my family was kicked out when my father was arrested when the war started. My sister Goli at the time was in Barcelona, which is about an eight-hour drive from Madrid. She was in school studying to be a doctor. My mom said that my father never made it through Tehran International Airport. He just disappeared. Her brothers were waiting for him to come on the other side as he arrived, but he never made it through the terminal. Right out of Europe, they took him. They got him on the tarmac, and he was gone.

My uncle called my mom and asked where my father was. He told her he never made it through, but she knew my father was on his flight. She contacted the airport and confirmed that. They knew something bad had happened.

When I learned my father was in prison, the stress grew. Everything got worse. I called my mother and sisters. I felt the urge to give everything up and go back to Iran to try to help my dad. They told me not to go. I was already in the United States. I was in the promised land. "Do your best to make something of yourself," my mother told me. " Go become successful and help to bring the rest of the family over."

Not knowing fully what happened at the time, my mother told me that one day there was a knock at their door. They were told that they had to leave the embassy. No reason was given as to why they had to pack up their bags and leave. They were literally thrown out onto the street. Nobody told her anything. With nowhere to go, they went to stay with Goli in Barcelona in her one-bedroom apartment.

When they got there, they realized they had no money, no savings. There was no secret bank account or any money. My mom never had dealt with money. My poor sister had to give up medical school. She became the sole supporter of the family. She became a street vendor. She'd go buy stuff and try to sell it on the streets. My other two sisters were too young to work at that time. Goli did this because she needed to make money. At the time, Iran was at war with Iraq, and Saddam Hussein used chemical weapons against the Iranian Kurdish people. They were using mustard gas and chemicals that were blinding the soldiers. A lot of these soldiers who were blinded were sent to Barcelona. They went to a clinic focused on eye care. They got their eyes examined and doctors tried to do what they could. They saw a lot of Iranian soldiers, young men maybe 16 or 18 years old, who'd lost their eyesight.

Somebody at the clinic asked my sister if she spoke Farsi, which she did. She became a translator there. The soldiers needed money, so my sister would buy stuff from them. She bought caviar, pistachios, and carpets. The poor soldiers who'd risked their lives for nothing would bring caviar to sell to pay for their medical bills. She saw the opportunity and she went on to sell Iranian caviar, which is some of the most famous in the world. This enterprise took off, and selling caviar became her main business. She'd buy from the soldiers and then sell to clients that eventually included fine hotels and restaurants. She'd walk in and tell them that she had better caviar than they had. And she did.

My other sister, Banafsheh, had a master's degree in civil engineering when she came to the United States, but she had to start from scratch. She got a job distributing newspapers and did that for a few months while converting all her degrees and education to U.S. standards. She kept working and taking courses and eventually got a government job in Sacramento County. She oversees all of California's water resources. I'm extremely proud of her and of my entire family. We're all extremely driven and successful and have been gifted life and perspective by our loving parents. Despite my own loneliness, I understood why my family couldn't be there throughout this time.

It took almost two and a half years to find out that my dad was alive and in prison. Nobody contacted my mother. Nobody had contacted my sister or any family members to say that he was in the custody of Iranian forces. I promised myself that I would bring them over to the U.S. to give them a better life. I'm proud to say that I succeeded in that and I'm proud to be a part of a family with such incredible perseverance.

Chapter 26

2020

It takes two years to find out what officially happened. The FAA, United, and the National Transportation Safety Board take their time with these things. They don't want to come to the wrong judgment. They keep the airplane in a protected hangar where inspectors from the FAA, NTSB, United, ALPA, Pratt & Whitney, and Boeing all have a chance to conduct inspections. Anybody that had anything to do with the part of the airplane that was damaged sends their own special team to come up with their own independent findings. They tell us six to nine months, but it ends up taking two and a half years.

Finally we learn what happened. Investigators conclude that a fan blade broke off during the flight, causing an engine failure and forcing our emergency landing. Pratt & Whitney's inspectors had failed to notice signs that the blade was weak in various spots. The NTSB said that the maker of the engine hadn't provided a formal program for training their inspectors who examined the fan blades. The safety board also found that the blade that had snapped off had shown previous signs of wear and tear from other examinations, but that it was wrongly believed to have been a paint imperfection.

The 777 had experienced a full-length fan blade fracture in the right engine shortly before the top of descent. *The Wall Street Journal* reported that the NTSB "concluded that a roughly 35-pound fan blade broke in the plane's Pratt & Whitney PW4000 engine due to fatigue, spiraling forward and causing parts of the engine cover to drop in the sea." By the time of landing, most of the inlet duct, and all of the left and right fan cowls, were missing and there were two small punctures on the right side of the fuselage below the window belt from hits from pieces of the engine fan blade. Two blades had fractured off. One was fractured transversely across the airfoil directly above the fairings that are between the base of each blade, and the other was fractured across the airfoil at about midspan.

Now, the fan blades in the engine were last overhauled in July 2015. They underwent Fluorescent Penetrant Inspection (FPI) and Thermal Acoustic Imaging (TAI) inspection. Records from then and from March 2010 showed that there was an "indication" in the same location where the crack had occurred. It was dismissed as "paint," but in reality it was a hairline crack. This differs from the records from the TAI inspection that had just noted paint. Pratt & Whitney had developed the TAI inspection process back in 2005 to inspect the interior surfaces of the fan blades. It was classified as a new and emerging technology, and because of this, they weren't required to develop a formal training program or certification process for inspectors. This is something that should have been done. In 2018, when the incident occurred, the inspection was still categorized as a new and emerging technology, even after having inspected over 9,000 blades. While Pratt & Whitney did offer training at one point on TAI, the two inspectors who'd inspected the blades on our plane hadn't been permitted to attend the training that day. They were made to work on clearing out a backlog of blades in the shop. On top of that, one of the inspectors who worked on the fan blade on the plane reported that they never received any feedback from the engineers about blades that had been rejected. While the blades would go to an engineer for evaluation, the original inspectors never received the knowledge of whether their rejection was valid or a false positive.

The National Transportation Safety Board ultimately concluded that the probable cause for this incident was due to Pratt & Whitney's continued classification of the inspection process as a new and emerging technology that led to a lack of training and an incorrect evaluation The result was that a blade with a crack in was returned to service that day. It fractured, endangering the lives of everyone on board. If something worse had happened—for example, if the blade had penetrated the fuselage or pierced a window—we all may have very well died that day.

Chapter 27

1987 – Present

My girlfriend, Beth, who would later become my wife and the mother of my children, went to San Diego for her master's degree. At the same time, I got hired by United and was shipped to Chicago as a flight engineer. Beth was in San Diego, pursuing her master's degree. We'd be a long-distance relationship for the next two years. My mother came out to America for the first time in 1988 while I was in Chicago. I'd already applied to be transferred to San Francisco, and I received my lateral bid from Chicago to San Francisco shortly before she arrived. So literally the day after she got into town, we drove from Chicago to Sacramento, where my cousin lived. I rented an apartment for my mother to stay in while I flew. A few months later, I bought my first house in Sacramento, and in September of 1990, Beth and I got married.

Chapter 27

I was living in Sacramento and commuting to San Francisco, flying as a flight engineer on a 747. It was an emotional day when I first sat in the cockpit of that 747. I was living my dream. My dream had come full circle, and it was mine. I thought about being a kid in Iran and watching the 747 take off. It was the beginning of a long, difficult journey. But that day, as I walked to the plane through Gate 80 at SFO, my senses were on hyperdrive. I had tears in my eyes. We took off from San Francisco to Honolulu (the retrospective symbolism does not escape me). My dream had been reached.

As I settled into becoming a pilot for United, I fell into a sort of malaise. I fell into a rhythm. I'd arrived, but I felt aimless. There had to be more. I asked myself if there was something bigger or more important in my life for me to accomplish. I found myself questioning where I was. I wasn't satisfied. I wanted to keep pushing myself. My career was on autopilot. I'd done everything I could possibly do to get into the system and once I was there, I had to keep my nose clean and go through it year after year, building up more seniority, my income stepping up each year. Initially, it wasn't that bad. When I was in a 747, I was a junior pilot and was on reserve. Some months I only flew one trip. I'd take a trip to Hong Kong or Australia or Tokyo for four days and then I'd have 26 days off.

But I was getting bored, and I was stuck on B-scale for the next five years due to how the negotiations ended up after the strike. This meant that at first, I was only making $1,800 a month. Eventually, though, it went up to $2,000, but it stayed like that for the five years, then jumped from $24,000 to $90,000 a year. But until then, I had to do something with all the time on my hands.

I got involved in real estate. I learned quickly and found a knack for it. By the age of 34, I'd become a millionaire. It was always a goal of mine. I enjoyed my job, but I wanted to get to a point in my life where I didn't have to work for a living, where I'd work because I loved my job, not because I was financially stuck to it.

I kept working. Shortly after Beth and I married, my mother went back to Iran. She wouldn't return until 1995, when she moved to America for good. Our family grew. In 1993 my first son, Matthew, was born, and two years later my wife and I welcomed another son, Alexander, into our lives. We were later blessed with two beautiful daughters, Susanna and Emma. We kept at it. Life's pattern continued. Real estate was still working. We were living the dream.

In 1994, my father came over to America for the first time. We finally had a chance to connect. It was eerie, yet absolutely wonderful, magical even. It had been so long since I'd seen him, and here I was a grown man with my father before me. He apologized for not being a good father and for being out of my life so much. This couldn't have been further from the truth. Everything I'd done was for him. The principles and values and my idea of what it means to be a man all came from him. I told him, "Absolutely not." I told him that I had great admiration for what he had done, not only for his family but also for his country. I told him that I understood the tragedy of the situation and I let him know that if I had grown up under different circumstances, I probably wouldn't have made it to the point in my life that I had.

We were able to reconnect. He told me again that his blood ran through my veins, that his strength was transferred to me, from one generation to another. He told me that when he was in prison, he told himself that he wasn't going to die because he wanted to see his only son again. I thought back to this while in the air struggling to land Flight 1175. The least I could do was land that plane. I made one decision that day. That day was not the day that we would die. I had not said my goodbyes to those who meant the most to me.

But my father wouldn't be able to stay for long. The government wanted him back. We didn't want him to leave, but my mother and my eldest sister, her kids, and her husband were still in Iran, and their lives might have been in danger if he didn't return. We didn't know if they were going to put him in jail, if they were going to kill him, just leave him alone, or put him under house arrest again. He told me that he wanted me to purchase a home for every single one of my sisters for when they came to America. With a very heavy heart we said goodbye in San Francisco. He left. He went to London, and from London to Iran, and I went to Denver to start my captain training on a 737.

Not knowing what was going to happen to my father during the first week of my training was horrible. It put a lot of stress and pressure on me. I felt a deep feeling of loss, a feeling of not being able to do anything about this situation. It was so overwhelming that all I could do was just survive and stand on my feet and keep pushing forward. Focus on my training and become the best captain I could be. Ultimately they just kept him in the country. They took his passport and wouldn't let him leave.

❋ ❋ ❋

Life continued. I found homes for my family and furnished them. I rented them out and told them that whenever they decide to come to America, they'd have roofs over their heads. They wouldn't have to start from nothing. I told them we'd help them get jobs when they came over. My wife and I, with the help of attorneys, got them over here. It was a promise that I'd made to my mother as a kid—that I would bring my family to America, not as refugees, but with green cards in hand. I was able to do just that. They've all found their own successes. I love them dearly.

In 1995, I made it to captain on a Boeing 737. With the promotion, I flew even more. For these first five years, I had time to manage all the properties, but once I made it to captain, I started earning more money and working a lot more. I went from being home 20-some days a month to only 12 or 13. I asked my wife to become more involved in managing the properties—picking up the rent, dealing with repairs, a whole range of jobs—but she didn't like it. Her heart wasn't in it. Life fell again into an ebb and flow until the real estate market crashed in 1998. The crash ricocheted through the whole state. A lot of investors in Sacramento pulled out of the market and properties dropped four or five times in value. It was difficult, if not impossible, to sell anything. I had to go out of pocket to sell my properties and I began covering the various fees and closing costs for buyers. I even had to sell my own house at a loss.

Given the market and our situation, my wife and I decided to move to Florida. I wanted the best for us, and we figured we should at least live in a place where we'd be happy. A dream of mine was to live on the water with a boat in the backyard, and United had a base in Miami, so it made sense.

We bought a house in Lighthouse Point, Fort Lauderdale, 30 minutes from Miami, and moved there with our then-three kids. Living in Florida cut down on my commute as well, which in California averaged about two hours if I didn't stay overnight on my boat. The silver lining to this period was that my father had made it back to the United States. I drove across the country to Florida with my father. We put my sailboat on the back of a trailer and drove it across the country for eight days.

It was wonderful to spend this time together. We shared a lot of stories of the past. He told me more about himself, stories of his imprisonment and the tortures they subjected him to. They played Russian roulette with him. They put electricity to his groin. It was humiliating, but he maintained composure, holding onto the knowledge and desire that he would see his son again. He told me that prison under the Shah's regime felt like a Holiday Inn compared to prison under the Ayatollah. Guards under the Shah had taken courses on how to be proper prison guards, but the Ayatollah's guards were essentially a bunch of thugs. It was incredibly emotional to hear all of this and see how much pain my father had endured. It was inspiring and heartbreaking all at once. I felt deeply that all I wanted to do was provide him with a good, comfortable, safe life, one where he doesn't have to worry about providing—one where he could simply live and do as he pleased.

※ ※ ※

In Florida, I was making good money. My wife and I were working at getting pregnant again. I was flying as the captain of a Boeing 767. Soon we had another daughter.

Early on during my time in Florida, I went to one of those bring-your-father-to-school events. There were firemen, policemen, businessmen—and there I was, this bald guy in a pilot's uniform. It went really well. Everybody had questions, and I was able to provide answers in ways some of the others couldn't. I found that a lot of teenagers were lost and needed a good role model. I shared my life story and perspective—from my dad being in prison, to my coming to this country from Iran without speaking a word of English. I stood in front of them, pumping my hands and jumping up and down and dancing and motivating them in a language that wasn't even my native tongue. I told them that if I could do it, they could do it too. Seeing that sparkle in their eyes when they got it was amazing. Afterward, there were hundreds of kids hugging me, asking me to take pictures with them, telling me that what I'd said had changed their lives.

After doing this first workshop in Florida, I started going to high schools and promoting United and flying. I read more books and listened to more audiotapes. These readings validated the pursuit of my accomplishments. They were talking my language. They were saying the same things I'd been feeling passionate about doing all these years. It was part of my DNA. I realized I had those seeds of greatness in me but I began to learn the language to express it so I could share my successes and setbacks and how I overcame them. I realized that I could convey these timeless lessons from the perspective of my own life story and experience.

As I began to do more and more motivational talks, my antennas were up to the real estate market. I could see what was going on in that area. There were a couple of developers coming in buying old houses, knocking them down, building mansions, and selling them for a hefty profit. At the time, my sister and a friend of mine wanted to invest, so we bought a couple of properties, and I started to build a portfolio in Florida. I bought more of my own and then found an investor who saw what I was doing. He just wanted a 12 percent return and didn't care about anything else. Things were going up. Each property was going up in value by 20 or 30 percent each month. Within three years I had 13 properties. It was becoming a force. I sold a few of them and I got almost $2 million of cash out. I became a millionaire again in my early 40s after losing it all in the previous crash.

I took this money and put it into a dream I've had since a child.

I'd always wanted to have my own airline. Because of the challenges United has had in the past, I wasn't sure if the job was going to be secure for the rest of my life. I wanted to have a plan B. So my wife and I started a commuter/charter airline that flew from Florida to the Bahamas. We had a Cessna 402C that we painted like a New York yellow cab with a checkered tail—like the model airplanes I'd painted yellow as a child in Iran. We called our business Yellow Air Taxi. Our motto was "Where can yellow take you?" I wanted people who had homes in the Bahamas to feel like getting a flight was as easy as hailing a cab. Things were going well. We were making money. I still flew for my first love, United, but we kept plugging away with our air taxi service. Life was incredible.

But then September 11 happened, and it threw us completely, as it did the rest of the world.

We had been airborne for over 11 hours that day, landing a Boeing 767 from Buenos Aires to JFK International, 30 minutes before the first aircraft hit one of the Twin Towers. I went to catch my commuter flight to Miami on American Airlines, but I was informed that there were no flights out of JFK because a plane had hit the World Trade Center. I'd thought that it must have been a small two- or four seat airplane. I asked the agent when the next flight was and was told that the airline was grounded. No flights were leaving JFK. The airport was shut down. I went to United's flight operation at JFK and saw that everybody was standing glued to the television. In horror, we watched the second airplane, a United Boeing 767, hit the south tower.

We knew at that time that this was a terrorist attack. I knew that the world would never be the same. A pilot who lived in New Jersey said that we could drive across the Hudson River from Manhattan to see what was going on. We talked among ourselves, wondering how the firefighters could get to the tops of the buildings. We watched the helicopters fly around the towers. I went to change the radio channel but heard a tremendous noise. I looked up to see the north tower fall. I cannot describe the emotions that I felt. It felt like my heart had been ripped out. Thirty minutes later, the second tower came down. My friend dropped me off in my apartment in Queens, New York, and for the next three days, we were glued to the television and wondering what was going to happen next.

I tried to call my wife, but I couldn't get through. Nothing but a busy signal. There was no way for me to tell her I was okay. Realizing she must have gone into panic mode made it all the worse. She had no idea where I was, other than I was flying into New York and was supposed to catch another flight home.

I kept trying to call.

No luck.

Word came that another jet was commandeered by terrorists over Pennsylvania. It felt like living in a war zone. We didn't know when or where we'd be hit next. A short time later, I heard that United Flight 93 was taken out by four Al Qaeda terrorists and crashed into a field in Somerset County, Pennsylvania. Instantly, I thought about Beth and how terrified she must be. We didn't know if we were under a big attack or what the situation truly was. The news just kept getting worse. I found out a short time later that I knew the copilot on Flight 93. We'd flown together, and he was a terrific guy. His name was Leroy Homer Jr. He was a wonderful man.

Flight 93 was different from the other flights. Melodie Homer, Leroy's widow, spoke about that day. She said that the reports that the flight crew was passive were wrong. Homer was the only pilot of the three planes that were hijacked who got off a Mayday call. Melodie has spoken openly about the layout of the 757 and the cockpit and has doubted the narrative that passengers used a beverage cart to break down the door. The cockpit voice recorder clearly showed that, unlike the news reports and purported narratives, the crew was not killed immediately. Pilot Jason Dahl was the captain that day. Melodie believes that either Dahl or Homer sabotaged the flight controls. According to the voice recorder, the terrorists were not able to handle the 757 at all. When Melodie got the word that morning about the attacks, she had a conversation with a United Airlines receptionist who told her, "I promise you everything is okay."

At the time, I wondered if my wife was in touch with United and what she might have been told. Still, there was no phone reception. Communication was jammed. The ominous busy signal made me sick.

We learned from calls received from passengers on Flight 93 that the terrorists had killed the pilots and were in control of the plane. Homer was an Air Force veteran, who, like me, longed to be a pilot from an early age. It was not lost to me that day that I could have been on that flight. I could have been killed. The small consolation was that my friend died doing what he loved.

I truly believe that those two pilots did everything they could to save the lives of the passengers, just as the American Airlines pilots must have done. Life changed for me that day, as it did for most Americans. My wife viewed my flying much differently from that day forward. So did I. Homer left behind an infant daughter whom he cherished. My thoughts gravitated to my wife and kids and what would have happened to them had I been on board that flight. For those pilots, crew, passengers, and their families, their hopes and dreams crashed into that field with them. The impact not only left a crater in that field but also in the hearts of all concerned.

❖ ❖ ❖

I had to pilot a flight on September 14, from JFK to LAX. My flight was one of the first out of JFK after 9/11. Only seven passengers were on board. It was eerie. That didn't even encompass the feelings I had. I wondered about the future of aviation, of my career, and all the what-ifs that rose to the surface that day.

On the descent to LAX, I couldn't clear my ears. I'd stayed up for four days glued to the television after my all-nighter from Buenos Aires on September 11. I'd caught a cold or virus that caused fluid in my ears. The flight doctor told me I wasn't to fly. The risk to my eardrums was too great, and I was grounded. It took me two weeks to make it home to my wife and kids.

Those two weeks were the longest in my life. Thoughts of 9/11 lingered. Even today, they are there—not as vivid, but nevertheless present. Yet life goes on. We grow and try to build the best life we can for our families and ourselves.

Life after 9/11 changed, and the aviation industry took these changes on the chin. The days immediately following the events, the government closed airports. Flights were canceled, and the airlines had to absorb the losses. Even after the airports were reopened and flights resumed, airlines across the board were hit by a 30 percent reduction in passengers. Most of the passengers who continued to fly had to for the sake of business. But many employers banned their employees from flying and kept that enforced for an extended period. The business dynamic changed dramatically. Congress was quick to act. Seeing the writing on the wall for airlines following the attacks, they passed a law and established the Airline Transportation Stabilization Board. The Board intended to give $10 billion in loans to the faltering airlines to keep them going. The ripple effect continued for some time. It turned out that the loans didn't help the airlines as expected. Bankruptcy and huge layoffs loomed. Wall Street held its breath. The world watched and waited. As a pilot, it was dreadful. With a family to feed and no promise of continued employment or income, it was an agonizing time. I had to think positively. I had to keep going. Like everyone else, we had to envision surviving the economic tidal wave that had hit the United States. United Airlines was at risk of going under. All the airlines were on the verge of folding. No other sector in the economy was hit as hard. It could easily have been a death sentence.

Then we got word that United would be cutting its workforce by more than half. Those who stayed would have to take a 50 percent pay cut. We lost a ton of money. I thought we'd be okay. We were still running our commuter airline out of Florida. Although I knew things might get rough, I felt strongly that our company would still be able to keep going. My wife and I dug in. We managed to turn things around and break even again, but when the Iraq War started in 2003, the price of fuel to fly our plane went from $2 a gallon to over $6. At the time we were burning 200,000 gallons of fuel a year, so that was $800,000 of potential profit that evaporated into thin air.

We struggled for two or three years trying to keep things going. We were losing the battle and as it turned out, we were on the verge of losing the war. The stress hit our marriage right between the eyes. We were at odds. We loved each other dearly, but the hardships and the byproducts of the siege prove too much for us. Maintaining Yellow Air Taxi became an uphill battle. People stopped traveling. It felt like I was rolling a peanut up Mount Everest with my nose. Our marriage continued to suffer as we got into more and more debt trying to keep the company going. We did what we could to save the company. I used money from real estate to invest in the business. We put almost $2 million into it. We tried our best to keep it moving forward.

The FAA still loved us. Our engine time between overhauls was 1,600 hours because our safety was so good. We never had an engine shut down. We never had an emergency. We did so well that they gave us an extra 100 hours each year. We went from 1,600 to 1,700 to 1,800, 1,900, 2,000 hours. That's an extra 400 hours for each engine, and each airplane has two engines, so we were able to fly more and more.

We were doing well and treating our customers right. We had six airplanes and 54 employees. We flew to the Bahamas, the Keys, and Sarasota. We were working incredibly hard to keep everything going. I had a full-time job at United. Beth worked full-time on Yellow Air Taxi and was the mother to our four kids.

But the crash of 2008 and worldwide financial meltdown was when the money really started to dry up. It proved to be too much for the business and our marriage. People didn't have the money for leisure travel. They were worried if they'd be able to keep a roof over their heads. Our load factor went down, and the work continued to weigh on my wife. We shut the business down in 2011. It was incredibly difficult, but I was able to close it on my terms. People wanted to buy the certificate to take over, but I didn't want that. I turned in the certificate to the FAA and did the best I could to move on with my life.

Three years later, we decided to leave Florida and go back to California to be closer to our parents. My wife and I would end up getting a divorce. She is a wonderful woman and a great mother, but we decided to go our separate ways. It all put too much stress on our marriage and friendship, and I learned to never again get my significant other involved in business with me. I had learned my lesson. It was a difficult divorce, and it took over three years to finalize. I'm grateful for the time we spent together and our four wonderful kids.

Beth and I have a cordial relationship to this day. I have nothing but praise for her. I wish things could have been different, but it is what it is. We all have our ups and our days. I think we both regret what we did. The failure of my marriage was a tough blow, but I was a survivor. It was as a result of the trauma of our divorce that I decided to improve myself. I had to keep growing despite the troubling circumstances. I kept striving to become a better person and to help people around me. I continued to stay a positive trailblazer. I taught my kids to visualize what they wanted to do. I'm proud to say that from a very young age, all our children knew what they wanted in life.

One of our sons is a pilot and the other is a doctor. Of my daughters is in law school to become an attorney, and the youngest is studying marine biology. They all knew what they wanted to do, and I'm very happy.

※ ※ ※

As I consider the future, I see endless possibilities. I feel compelled to give back to the world that has brought me so many blessings. I've become an advocate for the rights of women and children in Iran. I consider setting up flying hospitals to take to areas in the world that lack adequate access to healthcare. In my extensive travels, now over 15 million miles, the thing that really gets to me is the poverty in the world. Poverty eats away at a person's dignity and leads to terrible illnesses and neglect. I truly want to change that. This problem is so pervasive that countless men, women, and children are left weakened with nowhere to turn. Nothing is worse than watching your own children when they're sick. I consider how these flying hospitals could fly in doctors, nurses, and support staff and provide remarkable care for the poor around the world. Perhaps one day they could go to Iran. Children, anyone, dying due to lack of medical care is a horrible thing, and it doesn't need to happen. I grew up in Iran and was blessed to be raised by a loving family. No one would have expected that I, coming from a family in Iran of modest means, would end up where I have. It's a blessing from the Creator. I've been blessed to be granted more time in my life and so were all the passengers on that flight that fateful day. My life has changed dramatically. From the moment of the accident, I've reflected on my life, my future. I will never take life for granted. I have only succeeded because of my dear parents. My father was a dedicated man who strove tirelessly for the values which he believed in. He guided me and helped shape me into the man I am today, one who believes in integrity, honor, and duty. All my life I've strived to embody my father's principles and to be the man he wanted me to be. Every good deed I've done has been because of his love and guidance. I love him dearly. I'm grateful for my mother for her sweet inspiration and unconditional love and support. She has given me so much courage, even at a young age—the courage to venture out of Iran on the journey that would lead me to the United States. Without her love, I wouldn't be alive today.

❊ ❊ ❊

Our children are our future. I've been blessed with four remarkable ones. They have what they need and most of what they want. They're healthy and happy. As a parent, that's a tremendous blessing. I can't imagine the heartbreak of parents should their child or children become gravely ill. Flying as I do, I'm exposed to other cultures continually. I've found that people everywhere have the same needs, the same goals, and desires. There's no real difference except in zip codes. Relating to people on a one-to-one basis is the answer. If we get to know one another, we're less likely to view someone as an enemy. We shouldn't be so quick to cast stones at people. Instead, we should look within ourselves to eliminate our own faults. Reaching across borders, neighborhoods, and between people will help to eliminate prejudices, hatred, and ill will toward one another. I am a life-enhancer, someone who wishes to help other people, someone who is committed to helping other people reach and achieve their goals and dreams. That is a driving force in my life.

❈ ❈ ❈

I take a trip to Tahoe. My son comes up for the day. We take the boat out onto the lake. My beautiful girlfriend is beside me. The sun is shining. The wind washes over my face as we head out across the Lake. I'm going to live until I'm 102. I've decided that. I want to be sitting in my rocking chair on the porch of my log cabin in Tahoe or Alaska looking back at my life saying, "Yep. That was it. No regrets. I did this. I did that." I want to be totally used up when I die.

We continue out across the lake. My loved ones are

around me, and in my heart, I know that if I don't wake up that next morning, I'll have no regrets. I'll have lived a life worth living. Children are a message that we send to the future we never see. It is essential to ask ourselves: What message are *we* sending?

Epilogue

My Message: Do Not Delay Joy

When I sent 300 résumés around the globe, I had no idea who would hire me. It could have been an airline in Europe, the Middle East, or Africa. Wherever it might have been, I would have flown. It was so hard to live and get my education in the United States. I would have gone anywhere in the world to obtain experience. But I would have come back. Be it after six months or a year, I would have come back to the United States to continue my journey because my journey was clear from the onset. I would become a pilot for United Airlines in San Francisco flying a 747. That was my mission. And it was still my mission when I arrived back in California from Florida. My divorce tears me apart, but I get through it. I build myself back up. I still have my passion for flight and for life. I have my family. I have my health. I'm okay.

My friend Steve always says that everything you've built in your life, you've built yourself, not with anybody else. Of course, you've likely had help along the way. But you've built those helpful relationships. When the going gets tough, remember that you can do it again and build it back up.

❊ ❊ ❊

Life has its rhythms. There are exciting times, happy times, times of pain, and times of sadness. Sometimes things feel uniform and unchanging. But no matter what, life keeps going. We must make the most out of each day. That's not to say it's easy. There will be difficult times, and it takes work to stay positive. I encourage you to regard what one might call "failures" to not be failures, but mistakes to grow from, opportunities to learn. There is no such thing as failure. There are only minor setbacks. You are never defeated in this life unless you accept defeat. If we change the meaning of the word "failure," we can change the world.

Just as a towering oak started from one seed planted in the darkness of the earth, so does our brain. Plant a seed of growth, not a rock of failure. When we learn something new or have a new idea or perspective, we plant a seed in the darkness of our brain. There it is protected. We water it and fertilize it, and over time it grows. But eventually there comes the point that the area protecting it is too small. The seed needs to break through the earth and feel the sun. It will have to withstand the rain and the sleet and sun and storms. It will survive winters and flourish in the summers. Growth is difficult, but it's a necessity in life.

It's like the example of a chicken in an egg. You might think of yourself as a chicken forming in an eggshell. The shell itself is your life support system. If the egg breaks, you'll die. But as you grow, the egg that's protecting you will begin to suffocate you, and that same environment that nurtured you will begin to kill you. What you must to do survive is to break through out of the shell to a new environment and grow.

This is what happens to us as we go through the different levels of our lives. We break through and become a bigger, better person. Physically, there's a limit to how large you can grow, but mentally there's no limit. Spiritually, emotionally, financially, there is no limit. You will always succeed if your determination is strong. A burning desire to reach your goals is the catalyst that will make them attainable. If you are anxious that you have not yet discovered something you are passionate about, be it a job or hobby that you find immense pleasure in, that's okay. Not everyone knows what their burning passion is at a young age. But you can still get there, regardless of how old you are. It's never too late. Try different things. Try new things. Explore. Keep searching. Keep asking questions. Dig deeper. Seek out the *why*. If you don't get the answer you want, look for another answer. Try a different approach. Keep doing it and doing it and doing it and you will get closer to your goal. Be patient. It's like the old saying: A journey of a thousand miles starts with the first step. If you wait six months to take that step, it's still a journey of a thousand miles. All you've lost is time. But once you're on that road, and once you start building momentum, you can imagine and visualize anything you want. Ask yourself who you want to become, what kind of person you want to be, who you want to meet, how much money you want to make, and how many places you want to visit. There is such satisfaction in checking off the boxes of your achievements.

Once you discover what sets a fire of passion in your heart, pursue it. That passion will go from your heart to your gut, lighting a fire in your belly that will never go out. That burning desire will become a passion. You don't even have to start with your big "passion" to create that feeling of progress. It can start with little things, like a checklist you take to the grocery store, or a list of chores that need to be done around the house. Just build a list, no matter how silly it may seem. Write your goals down. Put them on an index card and stick it on your bathroom mirror. Read it in the morning, noon, and night, and start checking things off. As you do, as you check your goals off your list as you achieve them, the momentum will grow.

Taking any action is better than none. Define your mission, no matter how small it is, and take massive, massive action to get there. A hundred percent is not enough. If you shoot for 100 percent, you're settling for 70 or 80 percent. Just to pass is not good enough. At 36,000 feet, when peoples' lives depend on it, you don't want a 70-percenter pilot. You've got to give it a thousand percent. Everything you've got. That way if you fall short, you're still over 100. As your momentum builds and builds, it'll get to the point where you don't care what it takes—you're going to do it and you're going to make it happen. You will see the *how*, like how Moses parted the ocean. The path will become clear when you find the *why*.

Some people I speak with while coaching have no ambition, no magnetic compass, nothing pulling them forward. I talk with them and guide them. Everyone's goals can be different, but, at the same time, everyone wants to know how to get there. You've read this before, but it is so incredibly important that I want to leave you with this on your mind. The *how* is not important. Focus on the *why*.

Why do you want to cross the Pacific on a sailboat?

The *how* is already there. People have done it. But why is it important to you?

As you examine this and dig deeper, as you start peeling back the layers of the onion that is you and start focusing in, you start to discover the *why*. You start to examine the things that drive you, who you are, and what you want out of life. If you want a million dollars, great, but what does that million dollars represent to you? A nice house? Then what's next? Kids? You must know the reason *why* you want these things. Otherwise you're just checking off boxes for a reason external to yourself. Often someone wants a convertible because they think that it will bring them happiness. They think that it's the car that they really want. But frequently it's the feeling that the convertible gives them when they drive through the mountains with someone they love by their side.

My father taught me that we must keep going forward, never relenting, never relinquishing our goals. Too often people give up, not realizing that if they'd kept digging, kept trying just a little longer, success would be theirs. Persistence pays off. We are on a one-way ticket on this flight we call life. It's essential to make the best of it. It's never too late to start. It doesn't matter who you are or what religion you belong to, we are all on this Earth trying to make the most of it. We have the opportunity to experience heaven on Earth every day. Live for the now, not the next life. Do not delay joy. Even when you may feel you're at the lowest you can go, keep going. There is beauty all around you. Just lift up your head and look. Go to the mountains. Go outside and watch nature. Be aware of everything around you. The world is a marvelous place. I plan to enjoy every moment of it that I'm blessed with.

❉ ❉ ❉

Recently I was on vacation in Florida, relaxing on my boat with Maleah and my childhood friend Mahyar. Mahyar reminded me of a story from my childhood. It was back in 1976, just months before I left Iran. I had just gotten my driver's license and had been pressuring my parents to buy a car. My father had recently purchased a shiny brown Mitsubishi Galant with a beige interior. It was glorious. One day I had to take my mom to the hospital in Tehran. It was me, my mom, and Mahyar. We couldn't find parking when we got there. The streets were busy, so I ended up dropping my mom and Mahyar off in front of the hospital. I told them that I'd go find a parking space and wait for them.

I drove up and down the streets, waiting for someone to pull away. Finally I found a spot framed by big, beautiful oak trees not far from the hospital. I parked and hung out in the car. Maybe 30 minutes passed and they still hadn't come out, so I decided to lock the car and walk to the hospital.

As soon as I got to the lobby, I saw them sitting. She was still waiting to be seen by a doctor. Before I knew it, someone came into the lobby and announced that there was this brand-new car on the street that a tree had fallen on top of.

Poor guy, I thought. But Mahyar suggested I go and check on it.

It was my car.

Sure enough, the big old tree had fallen longitudinally from the hood to the back of the roof. The car was entirely crushed. If I had been inside, I would have been killed. I had just missed death. Something had told me to get out of the car and go inside. Within minutes, the tree fell and literally cut the car in half. I'd nearly died again.

I believe that we are all put on this earth for a reason. For me, those 40 minutes up there were a defining episode in my life. My purpose was to be there at that time, on that day, to save those souls. The fact that those people are walking on Earth because of our actions is tremendously gratifying. Everything I was put through led to that moment, whether it was balancing rocks or sailing—balancing the sails with the wind and nature—or doing martial arts, meditation, aerobatic flying. All of this came to assist me in making the right decisions so that we could save those passengers' lives as well as our own.

※ ※ ※

I will continue flying and living in California. I will spend time with my family. I will mourn the loss of an old relationship and I will find a new one, a new love, one who supports me and is along for this ride of life with me. We will meet at a coffee shop. Maleah. You've heard her name before, and when I lay my eyes on her, I will know that we will be together.

Life goes on.

I will dream of showing my children where their grandfather stood up to tyranny. I will dream of taking them to the mountains where I forged rivers and devoured freshly made ice cream. I will dream of a world that is in balance, where people are equal, taken care of, and able to live their lives in peace, no matter their race, nationality, sexuality, or religious belief. I will dream of taking my children to the airport in Mehrabad where my father once took me, where I first saw a 747 take off, where the dream that guided my life was ignited.

I will continue flying, and on February 13, 2018, I'll wake up on my boat in Sausalito. I will drive to San Francisco International Airport. I will board United Flight 1175 to Honolulu, and my life will change forever.

Life is a one-way ticket. Twenty-five years from now you will be more disappointed by the things you didn't do than those that you did. You never get a second chance at life. This is it. So get out there and live it. Give as much as you can. Dance as much as you can. Enjoy all that life and the world has to offer.

What are you waiting for?

About the Author

Captain Christopher Behnam

United Airlines 777 Captain and Iranian Human Rights Advocate

On a fateful day in 2018, Captain Behnam was flying a United Airlines Boeing 777 to Honolulu when it suffered catastrophic engine failure. Onboard were 381 souls. The 777 was virtually uncontrollable. Were it not for his amazing piloting skills, the plane would easily have been lost. His exceptional valor brought the plane safely to Honolulu. ALPA, the Air Line Pilot Association, recognized his heroic efforts and those of his copilot and first officer. They awarded Captain Behnam and his colleagues the Superior Airmanship Award, an award that has been bestowed only five times since the 1930s.

Captain Behnam is also a successful entrepreneur and businessman as well as a public figure and speaker, conducting leadership and motivational seminars.

Captain Behnam, who was born in Iran, is the founder of Help Free Iran, a U.S.-based nonprofit organization. The group aims to unite and collaborate with Iranians and non-Iranians alike in the effort to create a democratic Iran, free of authoritarian rule, corruption, inequality, economic turmoil, human rights violations, and religious doctrine.

Acknowledgments

In the face of a catastrophic engine failure and the harrowing emergency that ensued, I owe an immeasurable debt of gratitude to my courageous copilots and dedicated flight attendants. Their exceptional professionalism and composure during those critical moments saved lives and ensured the safety of everyone on board. I am in awe of their remarkable skills and dedication. I especially want to thank my copilots Paul Ayers and Ed Gagarin. Our extensive training and collective experience resulted in saving 381 lives.

I extend a profound thank-you to United Airlines for granting me the opportunity to pursue my dream of becoming a pilot. United's exceptional management and greatness as an airline have fostered an environment of growth and excellence. I am deeply grateful for the support and opportunities they have provided.

I believe we at United have the best training in this industry. Their training center creates the best and safest pilots. Our compliance with United's SOP (Standard Operating Procedure) made all the difference on Flight 1175.

To my cherished Mom and Dad—your constant support, boundless love, and giving nature have been pillars of strength throughout my journey. Your belief in my abilities has been a driving force behind my determination to succeed, and I am forever grateful for your presence in my life.

To my wonderful children, Matthew, Alexander, Susanna, and Emma: You are the source of my inspiration and the reason for my unwavering commitment to safety and excellence. Your smiles and love have been my motivation during both smooth skies and turbulent times, and I am blessed to have such awesome kids in my life.

To my beautiful girlfriend, Maleah—your support and understanding during the challenging moments of this journey have been a source of comfort and encouragement. Your presence by my side has made all the difference, and I am deeply thankful for your unwavering belief in me.

Special thanks go to Aaron Kitchen for his invaluable content input and organization, and to Bob Howells for his skilled copyediting of this book.

To each one of you, I extend my heartfelt appreciation for being an integral part of this journey. Your love and support have helped me overcome obstacles and reach new heights as a pilot and as a person. This book is a tribute to the collective efforts and love of all who have touched my life.

With deepest appreciation,
Captain Christopher Behnam

[Blurbs]

Praise for *A Date With Destiny*

Airline pilots train for events like those described on Flight 1175, but managing the unexpected and unprecedented takes a calm resolve that you can't teach. Captain Benham brought his training and these innate skills to bear in getting 1175 and its passengers on the ground safely.

—Marc Champion
Vice President – Flight Operations
United Airlines

This story encapsulates the essence of America, offering opportunities to an immigrant boy who possessed nothing but a burning desire to achieve his lifelong dream of becoming a pilot. It exemplifies resilience, unwavering determination, and the pursuit of excellence.

—David Khalaj
Entrepreneur and Realtor, Pro Sports Realty

Captain Behnam brilliantly led a novel crew, securing 381 lives. We prep for the improbable, and he aced it, embodying his profession's essence.

—Stan Snow
Retired Assistant Pilot, United Airlines
Director – Boeing Flight Training, Hawaiian Airlines

Captain Behnam will inspire you to find a deep purpose for living, to focus on those you serve, and to visualize the outcomes you seek. He reminds us that hope exists even in the face of seemingly insurmountable challenges, and that the concept of "impossible" is an illusion.

—Jacob Narayan
Executive Producer

This is not just a book for pilots, although every pilot should read it. It is a book for anyone seeking balance in their own lives—preparing for that moment when they are "figuratively tapped on the shoulder and offered the chance to do a very special thing."

—Dr. Tony Kern

www.ingramcontent.com/pod-product-compliance
Lightning Source LLC
Chambersburg PA
CBHW052135070526
44585CB00017B/1832